Digital Game Design

Maura Mengoni · Laura Cormio · Tommaso Santilli

Digital Game Design

Voices, Values and Visions

Springer

Maura Mengoni
Department of Industrial Engineering
and Mathematical Sciences (DIISM)
Polytechnic University of Marche
Ancona, Italy

Tommaso Santilli
Department of Education, Cultural Heritage
and Tourism (SFPCT)
University of Macerata
Macerata, Italy

Laura Cormio
Department of Industrial Engineering
and Mathematical Sciences (DIISM)
Polytechnic University of Marche
Ancona, Italy

Department of Humanities, Literature,
Cultural Heritage and Education Sciences
University of Foggia
Foggia, Italy

ISBN 978-3-032-23319-6 ISBN 978-3-032-23320-2 (eBook)
https://doi.org/10.1007/978-3-032-23320-2

This Springer imprint is published by the registered company Springer Nature Switzerland AG
The registered company address is: Gewerbestrasse 11, 6330 Cham, Switzerland

Foreword

How do we design games where people might express themselves, discuss civics, learn, laugh, and grow? We often take games for granted as frivolous or unnecessary, but then how do we explain how playing cards with our parents is like chicken soup when we're sick? Or how playing *Super Mario Brothers* with our children feels like deep, personal bonding, like passing on a hobby for the next generation? How do we explain that playing with faraway friends in an online game each night fosters camaraderie, or that practicing ethics by playing role-playing games in a classroom helps us to become critical thinkers? How do we note that even in games like *Fortnite, Minecraft, and Overwatch 2*, there are opportunities for civic engagement, creativity, and mentorship.

When we play with others, we are, in a sense, building new worlds with them. Games are dynamic possibility spaces where we aren't just passing through, but we might be hanging out, forming friendships, and connecting with others. We also might be playing within communities that are toxic, and filled with hate and harassment. Games are both a product of our culture, and a force that influences our culture. They are ethical systems where values are expressed, negotiated, and sometimes problematized. Games matter. Yet, most of the research on games have focused on the games themselves, rather than on centering the perspectives of the people who create them.

This volume, *Digital Game Design: Voices*, Values and Visions, helps us to shine the light on the design processes and mindsets behind the games. It focuses on how designers grapple with the difficult questions of how to make complex, living systems like games. It centers the voices of real designers, and how they think through the choices of how to make these playable worlds come alive. It also shares how game designers embed their values in their designs. For instance, how do they think through important questions like how to balance the different goals of the game, or how do they navigate logistical and technical constraints to make a game more accessible to all.

I thought deeply about these types of questions when I designed a game with the World Health Organization (WHO) called *My Five Moments: The Game*. In this game, you play as a doctor or nurse and help protect alien creatures by doing hand hygiene (cleaning your hands) at the right moment. This game, which trains real doctors and nurses, is impactful. It even helped to protect real patients against a Lassa Virus outbreak in Nigeria by training people at a hospital in the River States. When I was designing *My Five Moments*, I navigated many complex design decisions. For instance, we had to make difficult choices around ensuring that all people could play, no matter what type of Internet bandwidth they had, and also making sure that the game accurately simulated clinical steps and hospital spaces.

Games, and their designs, are not neutral. With every game mechanic, story, interface, accessibility option, and interaction that we use, we are affecting what is rewarded or incentivized, and who is valued in a game. Does your design support collaboration and challenge, or competitiveness and crafting? Is your community moderated by human mods or is it self-moderated by the players themselves? Is it accessible to all color blindness types, and on all different types of computer devices? Is it free? Each design and sociotechnical choice shapes whether players are included or excluded, whether they feel isolated or belongingness, and which players are seen or ignored. This volume shares the tacit knowledge, values, and viewpoints that designers might employ when making decisions on the games and worlds they create. It reveals the tensions that designers consider, such as between freedom and constraint, evolution and stasis, and intention and impact. It also shows how our biases might inadvertently show up in our designs.

Games, in this sense, are mirrors of who we are and who we hope to be. Games can be spaces where we might test out hypotheses of the type of world we want to live in, and ways we might redesign it to be more inclusive, caring, and compassionate. It also might show us what went wrong, and how spaces might have ended up filled with both good and bad behavior. As you read, I encourage you to think about the games that you play. What values do they embed? What ethics do you perform? What views or visions do they uphold? What other ways could these games have been designed? Ultimately, games are messy, deeply flawed, and human. There are no easy answers for how to design games. This volume helps to unpack this messiness and through its analysis, shows the importance and impact of games.

Karen Schrier
Marist University
Poughkeepsie, New York, USA

Acknowledgements

We would like to express our heartfelt gratitude to Professor **Catia Giaconi** and Professor **Vincenzo Maria Marcello La Matina**, both of the **University of Macerata, Italy**, for the intellectual generosity with which they accompanied some of the reflections developed in this volume. Professor Giaconi, as the doctoral supervisor of T.S. and President of the *Italian Society of Special Education*, offered invaluable guidance on the themes of inclusion and accessibility in digital games, helping us to deepen their educational and human significance. Professor La Matina, drawing on his expertise in the philosophy of language and semiotics, enriched our reflection on the role of games as forms of communication and artistic expression. Their contributions helped us sharpen our interpretive lens and broaden the conceptual reach of this work.

Our deepest thanks also go to all the **game designers** who agreed to take part in this research. Their willingness to open their creative worlds to us, to share their perspectives, and to explore with us the many layers of their design processes made this monograph possible. Through their voices, we gained access not only to the practical dimensions of game development, but also to the values, tensions, and visions that shape digital games as cultural and expressive forms.

This volume is also profoundly rooted in the academic environment from which the authors come: the **Polytechnic University of Marche**, where they found an intellectually fertile context, together with laboratories and facilities of excellence that supported the development of this study. More specifically, the questions that animate this monograph emerged within the broader educational experience fostered by the opening, in the 2021/2022 academic year, of the Bachelor's degree in Information Engineering for Video Games and Virtual Reality, the first program of its kind in Italy. The collaborative work carried out with students arriving from many different secondary schools across the country, and bringing with them diverse backgrounds, interests, and sensibilities, made increasingly evident the need to understand, interpret, and in some way govern the remarkable complexity that underlies both the development of digital games and the experience of playing them. In this sense, the teaching and research path surrounding that program offered not only the context, but also part of the inspiration, for the reflections collected here.

Finally, we wish to thank the entire **research team** at the Polytechnic University of Marche, coordinated by M.M., for the support, dialogue, and shared reflection that accompanied the development of this work. Their presence helped create the broader research environment in which this monograph could take shape, and provided an important space for discussion, especially in its early stages.

Contents

About the Authors

Maura Mengoni is an Associate Professor at the Polytechnic University of Marche (Italy), where she teaches Virtual Prototyping at the Faculty of Mechanical Engineering and User Experience at the Faculty of Information Engineering for Video Games and Virtual Reality. She leads the Virtual Prototyping research group and directs the Virtual Reality Laboratory. As an active member of the international scientific community, she serves on editorial boards of journals and conferences. Her research spans User-Centered design and User eXperience methodologies, Emotional Design, new paradigms of Human-Machine Interaction, and the development of advanced tools in Artificial Intelligence applied to Human Factors, Generative Design, and eXtended Reality technologies across industrial domains. Currently, her work focuses on affective computing and AI to create user-centric approaches for symbiotic human-machine interfaces, as well as XR systems for cultural heritage and education. She is the author of more than 170 publications in international journals and conference proceedings and has coordinated numerous national and European research projects. From 2007 to 2010, she was scientific advisor to the Italian CO-ENV consortium, and in 2019 she was appointed coordinator of the scientific committee on x-Reality technologies within the national TICHE cluster for cultural heritage valorization. Holder of five patents, she is also co-founder of two start-ups, reflecting her strong belief in the role of universities in fostering applied research and industrial innovation. She served on the Board of Directors of the academic spin-off Hyperlean and, in 2017, founded EMOJ, where she was president until 2020. EMOJ has been recognized among the top five women-led AI start-ups in Europe and the top ten in Italy by UniCredit StartLab and Bocconi University. In 2018, Wired named her among the 50 most influential people of the year.

Laura Cormio is a Ph.D. Candidate in Learning Sciences and Digital Technologies at Polytechnic University of Marche and Foggia University (Italy). She graduated in Architecture at Polytechnic University of Bari (Italy) in February 2022 and she became a licensed architect in August 2022. In March 2025, she completed a research stay at Hasselt University, where she studied how people experience architectural spaces. Her research interests include the impact of architectural design on individual well-being and performance, the design of learning environments, User Experience design, and the role of AI in the design process. She has already published in peer-reviewed journals such as Design Studies and Multimedia Tools and Applications. She has presented various research papers at international conferences on architectural design and game design.

Tommaso Santilli is a Ph.D. Candidate in Didactics and Special Pedagogy at University of Macerata (Italy). His main research interests concern: (1) inclusive educational technologies based on extended reality supports; (2) inclusive design principles and practices and co-design theories and approaches to promote the Quality of Life of people with disabilities; (3) development of pedagogically oriented solutions to promote inclusive processes within leisure contexts, with particular reference to cultural life participation. He has published widely in these topics across national and international scientific journals and books. He participates in national and international scientific projects and was speaker at several international conferences concerning the topics of disability, inclusion, and design.

Author Contributions

This monograph was conceived and developed as a genuinely collaborative endeavor. L.C. and T.S. conducted the interviews and collected the empirical material, with L.C. leading the methodological dimension of the study. M.M. critically framed the exploratory rationale of the volume, contributed to identifying its main research dimensions, shaped its overall structure, and oversaw both the revision process and the editorial coordination.

The interpretation of the findings was likewise the result of a shared effort. M.M., L.C., and T.S. jointly reflected on the game design process and collaboratively developed the final conceptual reading advanced in the monograph, with particular attention to the relationships among the different dimensions under investigation. Within this shared framework, M.M., L.C., and T.S. all contributed to the discussion of artistic expression in game design; L.C. developed the ethical perspective on game design, while T.S. focused on issues of accessibility and inclusion. M.M. also contributed to verifying the coherence and robustness of the results in relation to the overall structure of the volume. All authors contributed to the manuscript and approved the final version.

List of Figures

List of Tables

Chapter 1
Introduction

Abstract Digital games have become central cultural artefacts, influencing education, art, ethics, and social participation. Despite growing academic attention, research on game design has largely remained prescriptive, often overlooking how design is enacted in professional contexts. This chapter introduces Digital Games Design: Voices, Values and Visions, a volume that addresses this gap through a qualitative, practice-based investigation grounded in designers' narrations. Adopting a Grounded Theory methodology, the book reconstructs shared patterns, assumptions, and decision-making processes emerging from professional experience. The analysis is structured around three interconnected lenses: designers' voices, which reveal situated knowledge; values, which highlight artistic, ethical, and cultural dimensions embedded in design practice; and visions, which frame how designers imagine games, players, and their societal role. Additionally, the chapter outlines the structure of the volume, which examines design processes, artistic expression, ethical responsibility, and accessibility as interrelated dimensions of contemporary game design.

1.1 Why Digital Game Design?

In recent decades, digital games have progressively established themselves as one of the most pervasive and influential cultural forms of contemporary societies. Once confined to the sphere of leisure and entertainment, video games today permeate a wide range of domains, including education, health, art, ethics, accessibility, and social participation. As interactive digital artefacts, they combine technological systems, aesthetic languages, narrative structures, and human experiences, positioning themselves at the intersection of design, culture, and society. This growing relevance has been accompanied by an increasing scholarly interest in understanding digital games not only as products or systems, but as outcomes of complex design processes shaped by professional practices, values, and visions.

Within this evolving landscape, game design has progressively emerged as a legitimate object of academic inquiry. Research in game studies, design studies, and

M. Mengoni et al., *Digital Game Design*, https://doi.org/10.1007/978-3-032-23320-2_1

human–computer interaction has contributed to the development of theoretical frameworks, models, and tools aimed at systematising the principles of game creation. From early formal and pattern-based approaches to more recent human-centred, playcentric, and iterative models, scholars have sought to capture the specificity of game design as a design discipline. However, much of this literature has remained prescriptive or normative in nature, focusing on how games should be designed rather than on how design is actually enacted in professional contexts. As a result, the everyday practices, tacit knowledge, and situated decision-making processes of game designers have often remained at the margins of scientific investigation.

At the same time, contemporary debates increasingly recognise digital games as cultural objects with significant social, ethical, and political implications. Video games contribute to shaping imaginaries, mediating values, and enabling or constraining participation in cultural life. Questions concerning artistic expression, ethical responsibility, and accessibility have therefore become central to both academic and public discourse. Yet, these issues are frequently addressed from external or theoretical perspectives, with limited attention devoted to how designers themselves perceive, negotiate, and operationalise such dimensions within their professional practice. This distance between theory and practice constitutes a critical gap in current research, one that calls for approaches capable of reconnecting conceptual reflection with lived professional experience.

1.2 Theoretical and Methodological Background

Digital Games Design: Voices, Values and Visions emerges from this context and aims to contribute to the scientific understanding of video game design by foregrounding the perspectives of game designers. Rather than proposing a new normative model of game design, the volume adopts an exploratory and interpretative stance, grounded in the narrations of professionals working in the field. By listening to designers' voices and analysing their accounts through a qualitative, Grounded Theory–based methodology, the book seeks to reconstruct shared patterns, operational frameworks, and underlying assumptions that inform contemporary game design practices.

The rationale underlying this volume is rooted in a broader recognition of design as a reflective and situated practice. Design research has long highlighted how designers operate within conditions of uncertainty, negotiating ill-defined problems through iterative exploration and continuous reframing. Game design exemplifies these characteristics in particularly pronounced ways. Designers must balance creative intent with technical feasibility, artistic expression with market constraints, and personal visions with collaborative dynamics. Moreover, the interactive nature of games introduces an additional layer of complexity, as design decisions shape not only artefacts, but also experiences co-produced by players. Despite this complexity, much of the existing literature on game design continues to privilege abstract models or formal descriptions. While these contributions offer valuable insights, they often struggle to account for the messiness, contingency, and contextual embeddedness of professional practice. By contrast, qualitative approaches grounded in designers' experiences can illuminate how design thinking is enacted in situ, revealing the strategies, tensions, and compromises that characterise everyday work in the game industry.

In this sense, the volume aligns with a growing body of research that advocates for practice-based and bottom-up approaches to design studies. By treating designers' narrations as a primary source of knowledge, the book acknowledges professional experience as a legitimate epistemic resource. Designers are not merely implementers of theoretical frameworks; they are active knowledge producers whose reflections can inform and enrich theoretical understanding.

The three key terms articulated in the title of the volume—*voices*, *values*, and *visions*—function as interconnected analytical lenses that structure the book's contribution. *Voices* refers to the centrality of designers' narrations as a means of accessing professional knowledge. Through interviews, designers articulate how they understand their work, describe challenges, justify decisions, and reflect upon successes and failures. These voices are situated, partial, and subjective, yet they reveal shared understandings and recurring patterns that transcend individual experiences. By systematically analysing these narrations, the volume moves beyond anecdotal evidence to construct empirically grounded conceptual models. *Values* captures the normative dimensions embedded within game design practices. Design decisions inevitably reflect assumptions about players, representation, responsibility, and inclusion. Whether explicitly acknowledged or implicitly enacted, values shape how games are conceived and experienced. By examining themes such as artistic expression, ethical responsibility, and accessibility, the book explores how values are negotiated within professional practice, highlighting tensions between creative freedom and social accountability. *Visions* refers to the interpretative and forward-looking frameworks through which designers imagine games, players, and the role of digital games in society. Visions guide design thinking by framing what games are for, whom they address, and what kinds of experiences they aim to offer. These visions influence how designers navigate permanence and change, structure and flexibility, innovation and constraint. Understanding designers' visions therefore provides insight into the broader cultural and social imaginaries shaping contemporary game design. Together, these dimensions enable a holistic understanding of video game design as a socio-cultural practice, embedded in professional, institutional, and technological contexts.

A defining feature of this volume is its methodological commitment to qualitative research and Grounded Theory. As detailed in Chap. 2, the study employs semi-structured interviews with game designers and a systematic coding process to generate theory inductively from empirical data. This approach is particularly suited to contexts in which existing theoretical frameworks are limited or insufficient to capture the complexity of practice.

By adopting Grounded Theory, the volume positions itself within an interpretivist and constructivist epistemological tradition. Knowledge is understood as co-constructed through the interaction between researcher and participants, and theory is conceived as an emergent framework rather than a fixed explanatory system. This methodological choice allows the book to remain closely tied to professional practice while achieving conceptual abstraction.

Importantly, the methodological focus of the volume is not an end in itself. Rather, it serves as a means to address broader questions concerning how game design knowledge is produced, transmitted, and operationalised. By grounding analysis in real-world practices, the book offers insights that are relevant for researchers, educators, and practitioners alike.

1.3 Book Structure

The volume is organised as a sequence of interconnected chapters that progressively build a coherent and practice-based theoretical framework for understanding contemporary video game design. Each chapter addresses a specific dimension of game design while remaining conceptually linked to the others through a shared methodological approach and a common analytical focus on designers' voices, values, and visions. Rather than presenting isolated thematic contributions, the book is structured as a cumulative inquiry, in which each chapter both deepens a specific issue and contributes to the reconstruction of a broader interpretative model of video game design as a reflective professional practice.

Chapter 2 establishes the methodological and epistemological foundations of the volume. It introduces the qualitative research design underpinning the study and provides a detailed account of the adoption of Grounded Theory as the primary methodological framework. The chapter situates the research within broader traditions of qualitative inquiry, emphasising the value of interpretivist and constructivist approaches for investigating complex professional practices that cannot be adequately captured through predefined variables or purely quantitative measures. After outlining the objectives of the study, the chapter describes the data collection process, focusing on the use of semi-structured interviews as a privileged tool for accessing designers' professional experiences, reflections, and decision-making processes. Particular attention is devoted to the rationale behind methodological choices, including the structure of the interview protocol, the selection of participants through purposive sampling, and the strategies adopted to ensure rigour, transparency, and credibility in qualitative analysis. The chapter then presents the Grounded Theory coding process in detail, illustrating how open, axial, and selective coding were employed to move from raw empirical material to conceptual abstraction. In doing so, Chap. 2 clarifies how categories and core concepts emerged inductively from designers' narrations, rather than being imposed a priori. This methodological transparency is crucial for understanding the analytical logic that informs the subsequent chapters, as well as for situating the volume's contributions within contemporary debates on qualitative design research. By foregrounding methodological reflexivity, Chap. 2 not only supports the validity of the findings presented in the book, but also positions the volume as a methodological contribution to the study of game design, demonstrating the relevance of Grounded Theory for exploring professional practices in creative and technologically mediated fields.

Chapter 3 addresses the game design process by focusing on how designers conceptualise and enact design thinking in their everyday professional practice. Rather than proposing a new normative or prescriptive model of game design, the chapter adopts a bottom-up perspective, reconstructing designers' approaches to design through the analysis of their experiences and reflections. Central to this chapter is the conceptual framework that interprets game design as a dynamic balance between permanence and change. Designers' narrations reveal how design processes are structured around recurring phases, shared routines, and stable conceptual anchors, while simultaneously remaining open to continuous transformation in response to emerging constraints, opportunities, and uncertainties. This tension between stability and flexibility is shown to be a defining characteristic of game design thinking, reflecting the complexity of designing interactive systems that evolve over extended development cycles. The chapter further explores how designers operationalise this balance through collaboration and iteration. Collaboration emerges as a fundamental strategy for maintaining coherence within multidisciplinary teams, enabling shared visions to be negotiated and sustained across different roles and competencies. Iteration, in turn, is analysed as a core mechanism through which designers test ideas, respond to feedback, and progressively refine gameplay experiences. By grounding these insights in empirical data, Chap. 3 contributes to bridging the gap between abstract design thinking frameworks and professional practice. It reframes game design as an adaptive and reflective process, in which knowledge is generated through action, dialogue, and continuous reassessment. This perspective has important implications not only for design theory, but also for education and professional training, suggesting the need to cultivate designers' capacity to navigate uncertainty rather than to follow rigid procedures.

Chapter 4 engages with the longstanding and often controversial debate on whether and when video games can be considered a form of art. While existing discussions on this topic have largely been conducted at a philosophical or theoretical level, this chapter introduces an empirical perspective by foregrounding game designers' views on artistic expression. After outlining the historical and theoretical background of the debate on video games as art, the chapter examines how designers themselves interpret the artistic potential of their work. Rather than adopting a binary stance, designers' perspectives reveal a nuanced understanding in which video games are not inherently artistic by definition, but may acquire artistic value under specific conditions. Through Grounded Theory analysis, the chapter reconstructs a conceptual model that distinguishes between the reasons why video games can be considered art and the ways in which artistic expression is uniquely embodied within the medium. Designers' narrations highlight elements such as creativity, narrative potential, emotional impact, and the integration of technological and artistic languages as central to the artistic dimension of games. At the same time, the chapter emphasises the role of player participation and interactivity in redefining traditional notions of authorship and aesthetic experience. By grounding the debate on games as art in professional practice, Chap. 4 contributes an original empirical dimension to a field often dominated by abstract speculation. It offers a practice-informed framework that helps clarify the conditions under which video games can be understood as artistic expressions, while also acknowledging the diversity of perspectives within the design community.

Chapter 5 explores ethical issues and responsibilities in game design, addressing a dimension that has become increasingly salient in both academic and public discourse. Digital games are recognised as powerful cultural objects capable of influencing behaviours, values, and social norms, and designers are increasingly called upon to reflect on the ethical implications of their work. The chapter begins by contextualising ethical concerns within the broader evolution of the digital games industry, highlighting issues such as violence, representation, monetisation models, and the social impact of games. Moving beyond player-centred or effect-based analyses, the chapter shifts the focus to designers' perspectives, investigating how ethical considerations are perceived and integrated into professional practice. Through qualitative analysis, Chap. 5 identifies a core conceptual framework that distinguishes between ethical issues embedded in the content and form of games, and ethical responsibilities attributed to designers, users, and other stakeholders. Designers' narrations reveal a complex negotiation between acknowledging ethical responsibility and preserving creative freedom. Ethics emerges not as a fixed set of rules, but as a situated and relational dimension of practice, shaped by intentions, constraints, and anticipated effects. By articulating these tensions, the chapter contributes to a more nuanced understanding of ethics in game design, highlighting designers' agency while resisting simplistic or moralistic interpretations. The findings have implications for professional ethics, design education, and policy discussions, suggesting the need for reflexive approaches that support ethical awareness without stifling creativity.

Chapter 6 addresses accessibility and inclusion by framing digital games as a significant domain of contemporary leisure with direct implications for quality of life and social participation. Drawing on perspectives from leisure studies, special pedagogy, and disability studies, the chapter situates game accessibility within broader debates on rights, inclusion, and cultural participation. The chapter examines how designers conceptualise and operationalise accessibility and inclusion in their professional practice, foregrounding their role as key agents in shaping inclusive digital leisure experiences. Through Grounded Theory analysis, Chap. 6 reconstructs a conceptual framework centred on the tension between facilitators and barriers to accessibility. Designers' narrations reveal how inclusive intentions coexist with structural, organisational, and economic constraints, producing a dynamic and often contradictory landscape. Accessibility emerges as both a conceptual value and an operational challenge, positioned between knowledge and practice. Designers recognise its importance and legitimacy, yet struggle to fully integrate inclusive principles within existing production contexts. Rather than presenting accessibility as a purely technical issue, the chapter highlights its cultural, ethical, and professional dimensions, emphasising the need for an intentional and reflective form of design agency. By focusing on designers' perspectives, Chap. 6 extends existing accessibility research beyond guidelines and technical solutions, offering insights into how inclusive design is negotiated in everyday practice. The chapter thus contributes to a more comprehensive understanding of accessibility as a dynamic process embedded within professional cultures and leisure systems.

Taken together, the chapters of this volume offer a multifaceted contribution to the study of digital game design. On a theoretical level, the book advances a practice-based understanding of game design, foregrounding designers' agency and highlighting the relational nature of design processes. On a methodological level, it demonstrates the value of Grounded Theory for investigating design practices in complex and evolving fields. On a practical level, it provides frameworks and insights that can inform education, professional training, and reflective practice.

More broadly, Digital Games Design: Voices, Values and Visions invites readers to reconsider game design as a culturally and socially embedded practice. By reconnecting theory and practice, and by amplifying the voices of designers, the volume contributes to a more reflexive, inclusive, and responsible understanding of digital game design in contemporary society.

Chapter 2
Experimental Protocol for Design Exploration

Abstract This chapter presents the methodological framework underpinning the study, outlining its objectives, research design, and analytical procedures. The research investigates how game design professionals conceptualise and enact their practices, with the aim of identifying recurring patterns and shared operational logics within the industry. To address this objective, the study adopts a qualitative approach based on semi-structured interviews with a purposive sample of eleven game design professionals. Grounded Theory is employed as the primary analytical methodology, enabling theory generation inductively from empirical data rather than testing predefined hypotheses. Data analysis follows a systematic coding process (i.e., open, axial, and selective coding) supported by qualitative analysis software, leading to the construction of a coherent, practice-based theoretical framework. The chapter situates this methodological choice within interpretivist and constructivist traditions, emphasising reflexivity, contextual sensitivity, and the co-construction of knowledge. By detailing the empirical setting, sampling strategy, data collection procedures, and coding phases, the chapter establishes methodological transparency and rigour.

2.1 Objectives, Materials and Methods

The study presented in this book was designed to investigate how game design professionals conceptualise and enact design practices in their everyday work, with the specific objective of identifying recurring patterns and shared operational approaches. To this end, the research employed a structured qualitative strategy based on semi-structured interviews, which allowed participants to articulate their experiences while ensuring consistency across the data.

Among the various qualitative analysis methods, we selected Grounded Theory to analyse the qualitative data gathered through the interviews, since this method is particularly suited for generating theory from empirical data rather than testing predefined hypotheses. Following the classic formulation by Corbin and Strauss (2015), the analysis was conducted through a three-stage coding process. In the first stage, *open coding*, interview transcripts were systematically examined and

M. Mengoni et al., *Digital Game Design*, https://doi.org/10.1007/978-3-032-23320-2_2

broken down into discrete units of meaning, which were labelled as codes to capture emerging concepts. During *axial coding*, these concepts were compared, organised, and grouped into higher-level categories, enabling the identification of relationships among them. Finally, *selective coding* focused on integrating the core categories and interpreting the emerging connections between them, ultimately guiding the development of a coherent theoretical framework that reflects shared design practices within the game industry.

The next two sections will, firstly, provide a general overview of qualitative research and, secondly, describe Grounded Theory in more detail, which is the method employed in this book.

2.2 Qualitative Research in a Nutshell

Qualitative research has long occupied a central place in scholarly inquiry across the social sciences, education, health, and related disciplines. Its enduring relevance lies in its capacity to shed light on all the aspects of social life that resist reduction to variables and numbers, such as personal experiences or interpretations. At a time when research is increasingly shaped by metrics, algorithms, and large-scale datasets, qualitative inquiry reminds us that social realities are lived, narrated, and understood by human actors embedded in specific cultural and historical settings (Burkholder et al., 2020; Lim, 2024; Oranga & Matere, 2023). Indeed, qualitative research does not seek to simplify complexity but to engage it, offering rich accounts of how people make sense of their worlds and act within them.

At its philosophical core, qualitative research is grounded in interpretivist and constructivist traditions, and it thus assumes that reality is not singular or fixed but multiple, socially produced, and continuously reshaped through interaction, language, and the creation of meaning.

From this perspective, knowledge does not exist as a fixed object awaiting discovery but is co-constructed through the relationship between researcher and participant (Oranga & Matere, 2023); accordingly, the researcher is positioned as an active presence within the research process, rather than as a neutral observer standing outside it. Reflexivity, ongoing attention to how positionality, assumptions, and context shape inquiry, is therefore not optional but foundational, and the researcher's presence becomes a resource for understanding rather than a source of contamination.

The purpose of qualitative research is, fundamentally, to understand phenomena as they occur in natural contexts. It is especially suited to situations in which little is known, where processes are unfolding, or where context is inseparable from meaning. Instead of isolating variables, qualitative inquiry attends to relationships, interactions, and the layered conditions under which social action takes place (Burkholder et al., 2020). In this way, it offers what has often been described as a holistic perspective: an effort to understand parts in relation to wholes and experiences in relation to the structures that shape them.

Within this broad orientation, qualitative research encompasses a range of methodological designs[1], each organised around a distinct analytic purpose. *Case study research* focuses on bounded systems, such as organisations, programmes, communities, or individuals, to understand how particular phenomena are enacted in specific contexts. *Ethnography* directs attention to culture, relying on prolonged engagement and immersion to interpret shared practices, norms, and meanings. *Phenomenology* seeks to articulate the essence of lived experience across individuals who share a common phenomenon, while *narrative inquiry* privileges stories as fundamental units through which people construct identity and continuity over time. *Grounded theory*, in contrast, is oriented toward inductive theory building, generating conceptual explanations of social processes through systematic and iterative analysis (Burkholder et al., 2020; Oranga & Matere, 2023).

What unites these diverse approaches is not a single method but a shared commitment to meaning, context, and interpretive depth. Data collection strategies[1], such as *interviews*, *observations*, and *document analysis*, are designed to preserve participants' voices and to capture social life as it is lived rather than abstracted. Analysis, in turn, is an interpretive craft. Through sustained engagement with the data, researchers identify patterns, relationships, and conceptual insights that deepen understanding rather than merely summarise information. While software tools may support organisation, the analytic work remains fundamentally human, reflexive, and theoretically informed (Oranga & Matere, 2023).

Concerns about rigour have often been raised in relation to qualitative research, particularly when judged by quantitative standards of validity and reliability. Yet rigour in qualitative inquiry takes a different form. It is achieved through methodological coherence, transparency, reflexivity, and systematic engagement with data (Lim, 2024). Strategies such as triangulation, member checking, audit trails, and peer dialogue enhance the credibility and trustworthiness of findings. Importantly, qualitative research does not seek statistical generalisation. Instead, it aims for transferability, producing rich, contextually grounded accounts that enable readers to assess the relevance of findings beyond the immediate study.

In contemporary research landscapes marked by rapid social, technological, and environmental change, the value of qualitative inquiry has become increasingly evident. Many emerging phenomena evolve faster than standardised instruments can be developed to measure them, and qualitative research, with its flexibility and responsiveness, offers valuable and unique tools to generate timely insights into such shifting realities (Lim, 2024).

2.3 Doing Grounded Theory

As mentioned above, Grounded Theory, as an exploratory and interpretative qualitative research methodology, differs fundamentally from deductive approaches. Rather than testing pre-existing theories, it aims to generate new theoretical insights directly from empirical data (Charmaz, 2014; De Smet et al., 2019; Strauss & Corbin, 1990).

Its distinctive strength lies in the systematic yet creative interplay between data collection and analysis, through which theory emerges inductively from the study of a specific phenomenon. This process of discovery, development, and provisional verification enables researchers to construct a theory that remains closely tied to observed practice, while retaining analytical rigour and conceptual abstraction (Hull, 2013).

At the core of Grounded Theory is the transition from rich description to theoretical explanation. This transition is accomplished through a structured process of coding and the hierarchical organisation of concepts into themes (Strauss & Corbin, 1990). Coding initiates interpretation by grouping segments of data under conceptual labels, allowing patterns and meanings to surface. This analytic process is inherently iterative and comparative: researchers continuously question the data, compare incidents, and refine conceptual definitions in order to generate increasingly abstract insights. Through this progressive structuring of concepts, a theory can be induced from the relationships that emerge among them (Hull, 2013).

In this context, theories are understood as an organised system of concepts and principles that explains, interprets, and predicts phenomena. It functions as a cognitive framework that enables researchers to make sense of complex realities by transforming empirical observations into abstract categories. When applied to design research, and specifically to the study of game design practices, Grounded Theory offers a methodological foundation for developing theory that is not merely descriptive but grounded in professional praxis. Here, it was employed to extract a theoretical framework capable of capturing designers' attitudes, workflows, and decision-making processes as they are enacted in everyday practice and articulated through interviews.

2.3.1 Empirical Settings and Data Collection

Among the various qualitative data sources available, including observation, document analysis, and quantitative material (Charmaz, 2014; Strauss & Corbin, 1990), interviews were selected as the primary source of data due to their capacity to capture professional experience in depth. As widely recognised in qualitative research, interviews are particularly effective in exploring complex practices, motivations, and reflections that are otherwise difficult to observe directly (Hull, 2013).

In this research, data were collected through semi-structured interviews using open-ended questions. This format ensured a balance between standardisation and flexibility: while all participants were presented with the same thematic structure, they were also given the opportunity to elaborate freely on their experiences and clarify specific aspects of their work. In total, the interview model consisted of 15 questions organised into six thematic sections, each aligned with the study's research questions and informed by relevant theoretical frameworks from the literature.

The first section focused on the collection of participants' background information. Section two addressed design workflows and working practices, with particular attention to how design approaches emerge through professional activity. Section three explored sources of inspiration and idea generation, drawing on existing research on creativity in design. Section four investigated the variables and constraints shaping the design process during development, such as team size, aesthetic decisions, user needs, ethical considerations, and external limitations. Section five examined designers' attitudes toward inclusion and accessibility, assessing how these concerns are integrated into design practices. Finally, the sixth section invited participants to share reflections on industry trends and professional experiences. A detailed overview of the interview questions is provided in Appendix A.

2.3.2 *Sample Characteristics*

The research involved a purposive sample (Patton, 2015) of 11 professionals working in the field of game design, selected to reflect a diversity of roles and professional backgrounds. The sample included eight men and three women, ranging in age from 20 to 50 years. While most participants were based in Italy, one interviewee was working in Bulgaria, contributing an international perspective.

Participants' educational backgrounds were heterogeneous: approximately half held professional degrees in disciplines related to game development, such as digital art, concept art, comics, or 3D modelling, while the remaining participants had completed either a master's degree or a high school diploma.

In terms of professional experience, more than half of the interviewees were early-career professionals, with up to three years of experience in the game design industry. The sample reflected a diverse range of roles within production and development, including business development managers, UX/UI designers, 3D artists, as well as other positions closely related to design and creative production. Ten of the participants were employed within game studios, while only one worked independently. Interviews were primarily conducted orally, with one interview completed in written form. To ensure anonymity, each participant was assigned an identification code consisting of the letter "P" followed by a number corresponding to the chronological order of the interviews. A summary of participants' demographic and professional characteristics is presented in Table 2.1.

Moreover, for each of them, an information sheet was created, encompassing not only demographic information but also the video games the designer was involved with, so that an overview of each participant is available. An example sheet is shown in Fig. 2.1.

2.3.3 *Data Collection & Coding Process*

Following the selection of the sample, the research team reached out to game designers via online platforms to invite their participation in interviews. These interviews were conducted either through video conferencing tools or in written format

Table 2.1 Participants overview

Code	Country	Gender (M/F)	Age	Education	Years of experience	Role	Affiliation	Interview format
P1	Italy	M	25–30	Professional degree	3	Business development manager	Studio 1	Oral
P2	Italy	M	30–35	Master's degree	10	Art director	Studio 1	Oral
P3	Italy	M	35–40	High school diploma	13	Lead game designer	Studio 2	Oral
P4	Italy	M	45–50	Professional degree	24	Project manager and art director	Studio 2	Oral
P5	Italy	M	25–30	Master's degree	6	UX/UI designer	Studio 2	Oral
P6	Bulgaria	M	30–35	Professional degree	12	Senior UX game designer	Studio 3	Oral
P7	Italy	F	25–30	Professional degree	3	3D Artist	Studio 4	Oral
P8	Italy	M	20–25	Professional degree	3	Animator/ technical artist	Studio 4	Oral
P9	Italy	M	20–25	High school diploma	3	Project manager/ game designer	Studio 5	Oral
P10	Italy	F	30–35	Master's degree	3	Project manager/ Game designer	No affiliation	Oral
P11	Italy	F	30–35	Master's degree	3	Game designer	Studio 6	Written

using collaborative software. Of the 11 individuals who agreed to participate, 10 opted for video interviews, while only one preferred the written format. Before starting the video sessions, participants were provided with a consent form outlining the terms of the recording, which they reviewed and signed. All interviews were subsequently transcribed from the audio and video recordings.

The data were analysed using Grounded Theory methodology, facilitated by MAXQDA, a qualitative research software. This approach enabled the identification of recurring themes and patterns within the designers' practices, offering nuanced insights into their experiences and perspectives.

The analytical process followed the classic Grounded Theory coding paradigm, consisting of *open*, *axial*, and *selective coding* (Strauss & Corbin, 1990). These three phases allowed to move systematically from fragmentation of data to theoretical

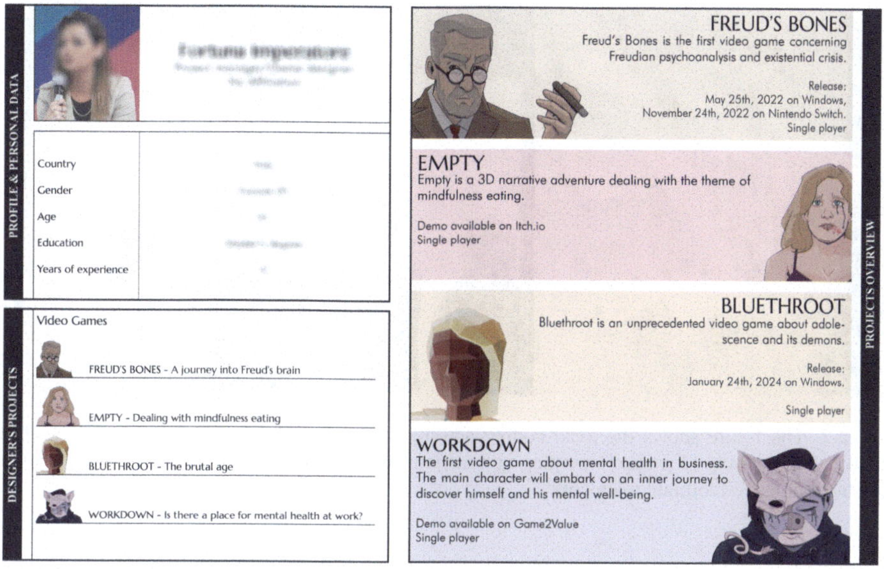

Fig. 2.1 Information sheet example of one of the interviewees, including the professional's personal details and an overview of the video games they have worked on

integration. Before starting, the transcripts and written responses were imported into MAXQDA for systematic analysis.

The initial stage of analysis was *Open coding,* during which data were examined line by line to identify concepts, along with their properties and dimensions. Concepts played a central role in this phase, as they operated on an ideational level that is fundamental to design thinking. Through inductive coding, it is possible to abstract from concrete statements to identify the essential elements of the phenomenon under investigation, thereby laying the groundwork for theory construction (Charmaz, 2014). Therefore, during this phase, the material was thoroughly read to extract segments pertinent to the research questions. These segments were then discussed collectively, and codes were assigned to emerging concepts, ideas, and thematic elements.

The process then progressed to an *Axial coding* phase. This phase builds on this foundation by reassembling the data around meaningful categories. The term "axial" reflects the analytical focus on organising categories around central axes of meaning, enabling a deeper understanding of how different elements of the phenomenon interact (Strauss & Corbin, 1990). During this stage, connections between concepts were collaboratively explored and articulated, seeking to establish thematic relationships among them. This involved examining the conditions, contexts, strategies, and consequences associated with each category. The categories were iteratively revised through group discussion until a shared understanding was reached (Fig. 2.2).

The final stage, *selective coding*, focused on identifying a central category that captured the core practices of game designers, the primary phenomenon under investigation, and provided coherence to the emerging theory. Researchers reviewed all

Fig. 2.2 The figure shows the axial coding activity, during which all members of the research team collaboratively identified emerging connections among concepts. All concepts were written on sticky notes to facilitate teamwork

previously established codes and categories, evaluating their relevance, frequency, and analytical weight. Once the core category was determined, its conceptual boundaries were further delineated by exploring its connections to other categories and subcategories. This phase thus represented the culmination of the analytical process, which transforms a set of interrelated categories into a unified theoretical model that accounts for the observed practices and meanings, as defined by Strauss and Corbin (1990).

Through this structured yet flexible process, Grounded Theory enables the development of empirically grounded explanations that remain sensitive to the complexity of professional practice while achieving conceptual abstraction. As such, it provides a robust methodological framework for investigating design processes and generating theory that is both analytically rigorous and deeply rooted in lived experience.

Notes

1. With regard to qualitative designs and strategies, please refer to the contribution by Burkholder, Cox, Crawford, and Hitchcock (2020), which provides an accurate description.

References

Burkholder, G. J., Cox, K. A., Crawford, L. M., & Hitchcock, J. H. (Eds.). (2019). *Research design and methods: An applied guide for the scholar-practitioner*. Sage Publications.

Charmaz, K. (2014). *Constructing grounded theory*. Sage.

Corbin, J. M., & Strauss, A. L. (2015). *Basics of qualitative research: Techniques and procedures for developing grounded theory* (4th ed.). Sage.

De Smet, M. M., Meganck, R., Van Nieuwenhove, K., Truijens, F. L., & Desmet, M. (2019). No change? A grounded theory analysis of depressed patients' perspectives on non-improvement in psychotherapy. *Frontiers in Psychology, 10*, 588.

Hull, S. (2013). *Doing grounded theory: Notes for the aspiring qualitative analyst.* University of Cape Town.

Lim, W. M. (2025). What is qualitative research? An overview and guidelines. *Australasian Marketing Journal, 33*(2), 199–229.

Oranga, J. & Matere, A. (2023). Qualitative research: Essence, types and advantages. *Open Access LibraryJournal.* 10, e11001.https://doi.org/10.4236/oalib.1111001.

Patton, M. Q. (2015). *Qualitative research & evaluation methods: integrating theory and practice.* Sage Publications.

Strauss, A., & Corbin, J. (1990). *Basics of qualitative research: Techniques and procedures for developing grounded theory.* Sage.

Chapter 3
Game Design Process

Abstract This chapter examines digital game design through the lens of design thinking, addressing the gap between prescriptive theoretical models and everyday professional practice. While existing frameworks have systematised key elements of game design, limited attention has been devoted to how designers actually navigate complexity, uncertainty, and contextual constraints. Drawing on empirical findings, the chapter interprets game design as a situated and dynamic process structured around the continuous negotiation between permanence and change. Permanence refers to stabilising elements such as recurring process steps and overarching design visions that provide coherence and direction. Change captures the variability introduced by market dynamics, technical constraints, stakeholder demands, and evolving team structures. Rather than positioning these dimensions as opposites, the chapter conceptualises design thinking as an ongoing balancing process, operationalised through collaboration and iteration. These strategies enable designers to maintain conceptual integrity while adapting to shifting conditions. By framing game design as a reflective practice grounded in adaptive balance, the chapter contributes to design theory and game studies, offering a practice-informed perspective with implications for research, professional development, and education.

3.1 Introduction: Design Thinking for Digital Games

The increasing cultural, economic, and technological relevance of digital games has progressively positioned game design as a legitimate object of scholarly inquiry. Once primarily discussed within professional or informal contexts, game design has gradually entered academic discourse as a complex design practice that intertwines creative exploration, technical development, and user experience construction. This shift reflects a broader evolution within design research, where attention has moved beyond artefacts as final outcomes toward the cognitive processes, practices, and decision-making strategies that underpin design activity (Cross, 1999).

Within this framework, the emergence of game studies as a recognised academic field has amplified the need for theoretical structures capable of accounting for the

M. Mengoni et al., *Digital Game Design*, https://doi.org/10.1007/978-3-032-23320-2_3

specificity of digital games. Early calls for such frameworks highlighted the risk of stagnation inherent in practices that rely exclusively on tacit knowledge and informal rules, without engaging in reflective theorisation (Church, 1999). Drawing on Alexander's (1964) distinction between unselfconscious and self-conscious design, game design can be interpreted as a field historically rooted in experiential knowledge, but increasingly oriented toward explicit reflection on its own processes. In this sense, the development of game design theory does not merely serve academic purposes; it also supports designers' ability to critically interrogate and evolve their practices.

Design thinking provides a particularly relevant lens for examining this evolution. Rather than describing design as a linear sequence of steps, design thinking focuses on how designers frame problems, navigate ambiguity, and iteratively construct solutions in response to complex and ill-defined challenges (Dorst, 2011; Gestwicki & McNely, 2012). This perspective is especially suited to digital game design, where outcomes cannot be fully anticipated in advance and where player interaction fundamentally shapes the final experience. Unlike static media such as books or films, games are defined by interactivity and by the player's capacity to influence unfolding events (Vorderer & Bryant, 2012). As a result, game design necessarily involves a degree of uncertainty that resists rigid planning and deterministic models.

Scholarly attempts to systematise game design knowledge have approached this complexity from multiple angles. Several contributions have focused on identifying the defining features of digital games and the elements designers must consider when shaping player experience. Church's (1999) Formal Abstract Design Tools (FADT), for instance, articulate core dimensions such as player intention, perceivable consequence, and narrative context as conceptual tools for analysing and designing games. Similarly, Björk et al.'s (2003) Game Design Patterns propose a pattern-based approach that identifies recurring structures and dynamics across games, allowing designers to reuse and adapt established solutions. The MDA framework introduced by Hunicke et al. (2004) further systematises game design by distinguishing between mechanics, dynamics, and aesthetics, thereby linking formal systems to experiential outcomes.

Alongside these discipline-specific frameworks, game design research has also drawn inspiration from broader design thinking models. Influential approaches such as IDEO's 3I model (Brown & Wyatt, 2010), the Double Diamond (Design Council, 2024), and human-centred models developed at the Hasso Plattner Institute emphasise iteration, user empathy, and the alternation between divergent and convergent phases. Although these models were not originally conceived for game design, their focus on exploration, prototyping, and testing resonates with established practices within the field (Fullerton, 2008; Salen & Zimmerman, 2004). In particular, the iterative nature of these frameworks mirrors the cyclical processes through which game designers refine gameplay, mechanics, and player experience.

Despite this growing body of literature, a persistent gap remains between theoretical prescriptions and professional practice. Much of the existing research articulates how games *should* be designed, often in the form of best practices or normative models, while offering limited insight into how designers actually work in everyday contexts (Martin, 2018). Empirical studies that investigate design activity across creative disciplines suggest that real-world design practices are often characterised by ambiguity, negotiation, and adaptation, rather than by strict adherence to formal methodologies (Crilly, 2015). In the context of game design, this discrepancy is further amplified by the diversity of production environments, team structures, and market conditions in which games are developed.

Reviews of empirical research on game development underline this complexity, highlighting the plurality of languages, practices, and organisational models adopted by designers (Berg Marklund et al., 2019). Flexibility frequently emerges as a defining characteristic of game design processes; however, it is sometimes interpreted as a lack of planning or methodological rigour. This interpretation risks oversimplifying designers' practices by opposing structure and improvisation as mutually exclusive alternatives. Instead, it suggests the need for interpretative frameworks capable of capturing how designers combine stability and adaptability in practice.

This chapter addresses this need by approaching game design thinking as a situated and dynamic process. Rather than proposing a new prescriptive model, it builds on existing theoretical contributions to interpret designers' practices through the lens of balance. Central to this perspective is the idea that game design unfolds through the continuous negotiation between elements of permanence, such as shared steps, guiding visions, and established tools, and forces of change arising from contextual, organisational, and market-related factors. This balance does not eliminate uncertainty, but enables designers to operate within it in a structured yet flexible manner.

By framing game design thinking as a process of balancing permanence and change, this chapter contributes to ongoing discussions on the relationship between theory and practice in design research. It situates digital game design within broader design thinking discourse while acknowledging its specific challenges, including interactivity, emergent gameplay, and extended development cycles. In doing so, it lays the conceptual groundwork for examining how designers translate abstract orientations into concrete practices, an issue that will be further explored in the following sections.

3.2 Balancing Permanence and Change

A close examination of game design practices reveals that designers constantly operate within a field of tension shaped by two opposing yet interdependent forces: permanence and change. These forces do not define alternative approaches to design, nor do they correspond to rigid methodological positions. Instead, they represent complementary orientations that designers mobilise throughout the development process in order to maintain coherence while responding to uncertainty. Understanding game design through this dynamic allows for a more nuanced interpretation of how design thinking is enacted in real-world contexts.

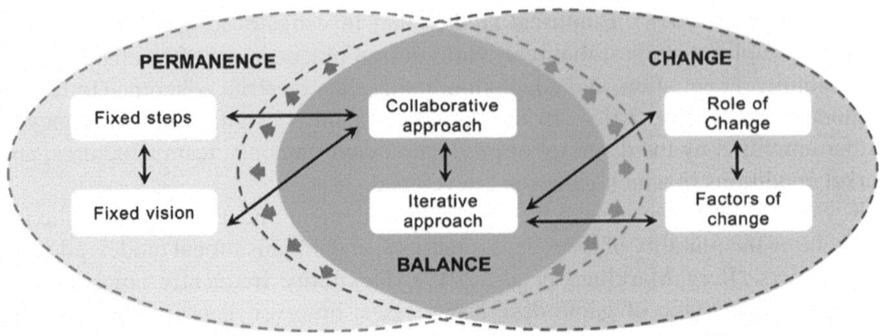

Fig. 3.1 Conceptual model of designers' attitudes and praxis. The model consists of three categories: "Permanence", "Change", and "Balance". "Permanence" and "Change" represent opposing yet interrelated forces, while "Balance" emerges from their intersection, mediating their coexistence through interconnected subcategories

The notion of balance is central to this perspective. Designers do not merely alternate between moments of stability and moments of disruption; rather, they continuously negotiate the relationship between fixed elements and variable conditions. This negotiation unfolds at multiple levels of the design process, from high-level conceptual framing to everyday decision-making. The resulting equilibrium is not static, but adaptive, reflecting both the situated nature of design activity and the evolving conditions under which digital games are produced (see Fig. 3.1).

Permanence refers to designers' tendency to establish and preserve elements of stability throughout the game design process (Table 3.1). These elements function as anchors that provide orientation, continuity, and coherence in a context otherwise characterised by complexity and unpredictability. Permanence does not imply rigidity; instead, it reflects the need for shared reference points that allow designers to align decisions over time.

One manifestation of permanence can be observed in the presence of recurring steps that structure the game design process. Across different projects and organisational contexts, designers tend to describe a sequence of core activities that frames development. These activities typically include an initial phase of concept definition and idea generation, followed by an assessment of feasibility that takes into account technical, economic, and market-related considerations. Planning activities often result in some form of documentation that supports coordination and decision-making, while subsequent phases involve design, prototyping, and testing in iterative cycles.

This structure resonates with established game design frameworks that emphasise iteration as a defining characteristic of the discipline (Fullerton, 2008; Salen & Zimmerman, 2004). At the same time, it extends these models by highlighting the importance of pre-design activities, such as research and feasibility analysis, which have been discussed in relation to game design documentation and planning practices (Almeida & da Silva, 2013; Neil, 2012). Although designers may adapt or rearrange

Table 3.1 Permanence

Sub-category	Code	Sub-code	Sentences	Number of participants
Fixed Steps	Pre-design	Conceiving and defining a concept	"Through a brainstorming among team members, […] design ideas are shared for a single project" (P9)	9 (82%)
		Analysing feasibility of the project	"First step is always research: have others done that? Is there something similar made outside the game industry?" (P6)	11 (100%)
	Planning the game development		"[…] a pre-production phase, in which the whole work is organised: we define the concept art, we decide what type of game we want" (P1)	7 (64%)
	Designing and prototyping		"Anyone involved can have an idea for a game and they can get people to start working on prototypes […] in order to see whether that idea really translates into a fun experience" (P6)	9 (82%)
	Testing		"I have completed this mechanic, now I have to send it to playtesters and see if they understand it, if they do what I want them to do as a designer" (P8)	9 (82%)
Fixed Vision	Starting from an overall view to progressively define smaller parts of the game		"You start from […] the hooks. The hook is what you need to sell the game. So, […] you need to start from there to build the fundamental aspects that embody it […]. Then you progressively proceed to work on the smaller parts" (P8)	8 (73%)
	Focusing of details first is counterproductive		"Focusing on the detail is what often jeopardises the project […], initially you surely must think with a wider view". (P1)	7 (64%)

these steps depending on the project, their persistence suggests the existence of a shared understanding of what constitutes the foundational architecture of the game design process.

Beyond procedural aspects, permanence is also embodied in what can be described as a fixed vision. Designers consistently emphasise the importance of articulating an overarching conceptual direction early in development. This vision typically encompasses the core idea of the game, the intended player experience, and the fundamental dynamics that define interaction and meaning. Rather than focusing immediately on isolated features or technical details, designers tend to prioritise a holistic framing that can guide subsequent decisions.

This approach aligns with Schön's (1983) conception of design as a reflective practice grounded in problem framing rather than problem solving. Framing involves defining what the problem is before attempting to solve it, thereby shaping the space of possible solutions (Dorst, 2011). In game design, this often translates into identifying core experiential goals, such as emotional tone, narrative direction, or player agency, that orient the entire project. Similar distinctions have been articulated in discussions of vertical versus horizontal design, where early attention to overall experience takes precedence over detailed system optimisation (Larsen, 2018).

Importantly, designers also recognise the risks associated with prematurely focusing on details. Excessive attention to isolated elements can fragment the project and undermine coherence, particularly in complex systems such as digital games. Maintaining a fixed vision therefore serves as a stabilising strategy that helps designers navigate the increasing specificity of development without losing sight of the broader design intent.

While permanence provides structure and orientation, change represents the equally pervasive dimension of variability that characterises game design practice (Table 3.2). Designers widely acknowledge that no project remains unchanged throughout its development. Instead, game design unfolds within a shifting landscape shaped by internal dynamics and external pressures, requiring continuous adaptation.

Change is first recognised as an intrinsic feature of design practice itself. Designers are aware that design approaches evolve over time, vary across teams, and adapt to different organisational cultures. This perspective challenges the notion of universally valid methods, emphasising instead the contextual nature of design practices. Flexibility is thus not merely a response to unforeseen events, but a foundational characteristic of how game design is conceptualised and enacted.

Moreover, change is frequently framed in positive terms. Rather than being perceived solely as a source of disruption, challenges and constraints are often interpreted as opportunities for creative exploration. This view resonates with broader design research that highlights the generative potential of constraints in open-ended problems (Kultima et al., 2016; Tseng et al., 2008). Within game design, limitations related to scope, resources, or themes can stimulate innovation by forcing designers to prioritise, simplify, or reinterpret initial ideas.

Table 3.2 Change

Sub-category	Code	Sub-code	Sentences	Number of participants
Role of Change	Considering that game design practices vary through time, among teams and among different approaches		"Another aspect is that each team works differently. For instance, our internal process changed through the years" (P9)	7 (64%)
	Highlighting the importance of flexibility of the game design process		"You never start from a fixed idea. If the solution does not work, you figure out something else" (P8)	4 (36%)
	Seeing challenges of game design as opportunities		"Not only design is easier when you have limitations, but in my opinion is also much more constructive" (P9)	11 (100%)
Factors of Change	Market		"[…] things can change, the game might take too long to make, and people have moved on. When *Fortnite* came out, games like that after it were too late […]. The market was already saturated." (P6)	7 (64%)
	Budget		"There are always limits […]: there will never be enough money […] and that is where lies the designers' ability, to make the most out of that mix of resources" (P2)	9 (82%)
	Time		"[…] maybe you can't make the characters speak to each other because you don't have time to develop that" (P8)	8 (73%)

(continued)

Table 3.2 (continued)

Sub-category	Code	Sub-code	Sentences	Number of participants
	Stakeholders' requests		"[...] also client's requests, that are often different from your vision. Especially in the initial phases." (P9)	4 (36%)
	Team composition		"It occurred to us to scrap two projects [...] the second one was not feasible for only two people to make." (P8)	5 (45%)

Several factors contribute to the emergence of change in game design projects. Market dynamics play a significant role, particularly given the extended development cycles typical of digital games. Shifts in player preferences, technological trends, or competitive landscapes may render initial assumptions obsolete, requiring designers to revise features or reposition the project (Karlsson et al., 2022). Economic constraints, including budget fluctuations, further impact decision-making by limiting available resources and influencing the scale and ambition of design solutions.

Time constraints constitute another critical factor. Delays, underestimated workloads, or evolving production schedules can necessitate the modification or abandonment of planned features. In addition, designers must often negotiate with stakeholders, such as publishers, clients, or target audiences, whose expectations may diverge from the original vision. Team composition also influences the trajectory of development, as the number of contributors and their respective skills shape what can realistically be achieved.

These factors collectively underscore the inherent unpredictability of game design. As noted in empirical studies of game development, variability and uncertainty are not anomalies but defining conditions of the field (Berg Marklund et al., 2019). However, interpreting flexibility as a lack of structure risks overlooking the sophisticated strategies designers employ to manage change without compromising coherence.

The interplay between permanence and change gives rise to a third, mediating dimension: balance. Balance does not represent a midpoint between two extremes, but an active process through which designers integrate stability and flexibility into coherent practices. This process is sustained through specific strategies that allow designers to preserve fixed elements while remaining responsive to evolving conditions (Table 3.3).

Two such strategies are particularly prominent: collaboration and iteration. Collaboration functions as a social and organisational mechanism that supports balance by enabling shared understanding and coordinated action. Game design

Table 3.3 Balance

Sub-category	Code	Sub-code	Sentences	Number of participants
Collaborative Approach	Importance of team communication		"People need to work together: games are not a one man show. It is really about the interactions and communications between people." (P6)	6 (55%)
	Importance of combining individual talents		"It is a matter of finding a balance together, in which everyone is capable of expressing their own creativity." (P1)	5 (45%)
	Sharing and preserving an overall view of the game		"We have a diverse team that still works in close contact in each phase of the work. […] everyone has to know how every aspect of the project will be developed and from who." (P11)	8 (73%)
Iterative Approach	Assessing design ideas		"What we want is a quick realistic feedback on our creative ideas." (P3)	8 (73%)
	Avoiding tunnel vision effects		"Each person tends to refine their field of work for love and for passion […] to the point of losing the overall view of the project […] it is a risk because it might create incoherence in the product." (P1)	4 (36%)

is inherently collaborative, involving professionals with diverse expertise who must align their contributions within a common framework. Effective communication allows teams to negotiate changes collectively, ensuring that adaptations remain consistent with the overarching vision.

Research on collaborative design highlights the importance of informal communication, shared mental models, and continuous knowledge exchange in supporting creative processes (Berg Marklund et al., 2019; Tran & Biddle, 2008). In game development contexts, collaboration helps mitigate the risk of fragmentation by fostering awareness of how individual decisions affect the project as a whole. At the same time, it creates space for individual creativity by allowing designers to contribute their expertise within a shared structure.

Iteration represents the second key strategy through which balance is enacted. Iterative cycles of prototyping, testing, and refinement allow designers to evaluate ideas incrementally, responding to feedback and constraints as they emerge. This approach reflects principles drawn from agile and iterative development models (Fagarasan et al., 2021; Kortmann & Harteveld, 2009) and has long been recognised as fundamental to game design due to the emergent nature of gameplay (Salen & Zimmerman, 2004).

Through iteration, designers can assess the feasibility and impact of design decisions without committing prematurely to fixed solutions. This process also helps prevent tunnel vision effects, whereby excessive focus on specific features leads to a loss of perspective on the overall project. By repeatedly revisiting and reassessing design choices, iteration supports both adaptability and coherence.

When considered together, collaboration and iteration illustrate how balance between permanence and change is operationalised in practice. Rather than resolving the tension between stability and variability, designers learn to work within it, developing practices that accommodate uncertainty while preserving direction. This balance-oriented perspective challenges simplistic representations of game design as either rigidly structured or entirely improvised, offering instead a more realistic account of design thinking as it unfolds in professional contexts.

3.2.1 Implications: From Perceptions to Practices

Interpreting game design through the lens of balance between permanence and change allows for a deeper understanding of how designers translate abstract orientations into concrete practices. Rather than adhering to fixed methodologies or relying solely on improvisation, designers appear to construct adaptive processes that integrate stability and flexibility in response to contextual demands. This perspective has important implications for design theory, professional practice, and education, as it reframes game design thinking as a situated and reflective activity.

From a theoretical standpoint, the framework of balancing permanence and change contributes to ongoing debates within design research concerning the relationship between structure and creativity. Prominent design thinking models describe design processes as iterative and non-linear, characterised by alternating phases of divergence and convergence (Brown & Wyatt, 2010; Design Council, 2024). The dynamics identified in game design practices closely resemble these models, particularly the Double Diamond, in which exploratory activities coexist with moments of definition and refinement. However, the present framework adds nuance by emphasising how these dynamics are not merely procedural, but deeply embedded in designers' attitudes and decision-making strategies.

The dimension of permanence sheds light on the role of structure in sustaining coherence throughout complex design processes. Designers' reliance on shared steps and fixed visions resonates with existing game design literature that underscores the importance of iteration, documentation, and early framing (Almeida & da Silva, 2013; Fullerton, 2008; Salen & Zimmerman, 2004). At the same time, the emphasis on maintaining an overarching vision aligns with broader design theory that conceptualises design as a process of framing problems rather than simply solving them (Dorst, 2011; Schön, 1983). In this sense, permanence does not constrain creativity; rather, it provides the conditions under which creative exploration can remain meaningful and directed.

The findings also suggest that permanence operates at different levels of abstraction. While fixed steps structure the temporal progression of design activities, fixed visions operate at a conceptual level, orienting decisions related to mechanics, dynamics, narrative, and player experience. These observations resonate with theoretical distinctions between holistic and detail-oriented design approaches, in which early attention to overall experience takes precedence over the optimisation of individual components (Larsen, 2018). By foregrounding these aspects, the framework highlights how designers actively construct coherence in systems characterised by high interdependence and emergent behaviour.

Conversely, the dimension of change foregrounds the pervasive influence of variability and uncertainty in game design. Designers' acknowledgment of change as an intrinsic feature of their practice challenges simplistic interpretations of flexibility as a lack of planning. Instead, flexibility emerges as a deliberate orientation that enables designers to cope with evolving constraints and opportunities. This interpretation aligns with empirical research on game development, which identifies variability, negotiation, and adaptation as defining features of professional practice (Berg Marklund et al., 2019).

The identification of multiple factors of change, including market dynamics, budgetary and temporal constraints, stakeholder demands, and team composition, underscores the socio-technical nature of game design. These factors correspond to dimensions discussed in the literature on design constraints and creativity, where limitations are often shown to stimulate innovation rather than inhibit it (Kultima et al., 2016; Tseng et al., 2008). In game design, constraints frequently prompt designers to reassess priorities, simplify systems, and explore alternative solutions, thereby contributing to the emergence of novel experiences.

Importantly, the framework does not position permanence and change as opposing forces to be resolved, but as dimensions to be mediated through practice. This mediation is captured by the dimension of balance, which elucidates how designers operationalise their attitudes through collaboration and iteration. Collaboration emerges as a central mechanism for maintaining coherence while accommodating diversity within teams. Previous research has shown that effective communication, shared mental models, and informal knowledge exchange play a crucial role in sustaining creativity and coordination in game development environments (Berg Marklund et al., 2019; Tran & Biddle, 2008). The present framework reinforces these findings by highlighting collaboration as a stabilising force that enables controlled adaptation.

Iteration, in turn, represents a foundational strategy for managing uncertainty in game design. Iterative cycles of prototyping, testing, and refinement allow designers to continuously evaluate design ideas against both conceptual intentions and practical constraints. This approach echoes principles of agile and iterative development models (Fagarasan et al., 2021; Kortmann & Harteveld, 2009) and has long been recognised as essential to game design due to the unpredictability of gameplay dynamics (Salen & Zimmerman, 2004). By engaging in iteration, designers transform uncertainty into a resource for learning, enabling incremental improvement and preventing tunnel vision effects that may arise from excessive focus on isolated features.

These strategies illustrate how designers enact balance not as a static equilibrium, but as an ongoing process of adjustment. This perspective challenges deterministic accounts of design methodology and instead positions game design thinking as a form of reflective practice, in which knowledge is generated through action, feedback, and reassessment (Schön, 1983). Designers are not passive recipients of frameworks; they actively interpret, adapt, and combine them in response to situated demands.

Beyond its theoretical contributions, this framework has practical implications for game design education and professional development. By foregrounding the coexistence of structure and flexibility, it suggests that teaching game design should move beyond the transmission of tools and techniques to foster adaptive mindsets. Developing the ability to frame problems, collaborate effectively, and iterate critically becomes as important as mastering specific software or formal models. Similarly, for practitioners, the framework offers a vocabulary for reflecting on their own practices, supporting more conscious decision-making in complex and uncertain contexts.

Finally, the framework opens avenues for further research. Future studies may explore how the balance between permanence and change varies across game genres, organisational settings, and cultural contexts, or how it evolves over designers' careers. Comparative analyses could also investigate whether similar dynamics emerge in other design disciplines characterised by high levels of interactivity and uncertainty. In this sense, the framework of balancing permanence and change should be understood not as a definitive model, but as an interpretative tool that contributes to an ongoing dialogue between theory and practice in game design research.

References

Alexander, C. (1964). *Notes on the synthesis of form.* Harvard University Press.

Almeida, M. S. O., & da Silva, F. S. C. (2013). A systematic review of game design methods and tools. In *Entertainment Computing—ICEC 2013* (pp. 17–29). Springer.

Berg Marklund, B., Engström, H., Hellkvist, M., & Backlund, P. (2019). What empirically based research tells us about game development. *The Computer Games Journal, 8*, 179–198.

Bjork, S., Lundgren, S., & Holopainen, J. (2003). Game design patterns. In *Proceedings of the DiGRA Conference.*

Brown, T., & Wyatt, J. (2010). Design thinking for social innovation. *Development Outreach, 12*(1), 29–43.

Church, D. (1999). Formal abstract design tools. *Game Developer Magazine, 3*(28), 44–50.

Design Council. (2024). *The Double Diamond: A universally accepted depiction of the design process.* https://www.designcouncil.org.uk/our-resources/the-double-diamond/

Crilly, N. (2015). Fixation and creativity in concept development: The attitudes and practices of expert designers. *Design Studies, 38*, 54–91.

Cross, N. (1999). Design research: A disciplined conversation. *Design Issues, 15*(2), 5–10.

Dorst, K. (2011). The core of "design thinking" and its application. *Design Studies, 32*(6), 521–532.

Fagarasan, C., Popa, O., Pisla, A., & Cristea, C. (2021). Agile, waterfall and iterative approach in information technology projects. *IOP Conference Series: Materials Science and Engineering, 1169*(1), Article 012025.

Fullerton, T. (2008). *Game design workshop: A playcentric approach to creating innovative games* (2nd ed.). Morgan Kaufmann.

Gestwicki, P., & McNely, B. (2012). A case study of a five-step design thinking process in educational game design. *Proceedings of the International Conference on the Foundations of Digital Games*, 1–8.

Hasso-Plattner-Institut. (n.d.). *The six phases of the Design Thinking process*. https://hpi.de/en/school-of-design-thinking/design-thinking/background/design-thinking-process.html

Hunicke, R., LeBlanc, M., & Zubek, R. (2004). MDA: A formal approach to game design and game research. In *Proceedings of the AAAI Workshop on Challenges in Game AI*.

Karlsson, T., Brusk, J., & Engström, H. (2022). Level design processes and challenges: A cross section of game development. *Games and Culture, 18*(6), 821–849.

Kortmann, R., & Harteveld, C. (2009). Agile game development: Lessons learned from software engineering. In *Proceedings of the 40th ISAGA Conference*.

Kultima, A., Alha, K., & Nummenmaa, T. (2016). Design constraints in game design: A survival mode game jam case. In *Proceedings of the International Conference on Game Jams, Hackathons, and Game Creation Events* (pp. 22–29).

Larsen, L. J. (2018). Juicing the game design process: Towards a content-centric framework for understanding and teaching game design in higher education. *Educational Media International, 55*(3), 231–254.

Martin, P. (2018). The intellectual structure of game research. *Game Studies, 18*(1).

Neil, K. (2012). Game design tools: Time to evaluate. In *Proceedings of DiGRA Nordic 2012*.

Ralph, P., & Monu, K. (2015). Toward a unified theory of digital games. *The Computer Games Journal, 4*, 81–100.

Salen, K., & Zimmerman, E. (2004). *Rules of play: Game design fundamentals*. MIT Press.

Schön, D. A. (1983). *The reflective practitioner: How professionals think in action*. Basic Books.

Tran, C., & Biddle, R. (2008). Collaboration in serious game development: A case study. In *Proceedings of the IEEE International Conference on Software Engineering and Education*.

Tseng, I., Moss, J., Cagan, J., & Kotovsky, K. (2008). The role of timing and analogical reasoning in design creativity. *Design Studies, 29*(4), 341–357.

Vorderer, P., & Bryant, J. (2012). *Playing video games: Motives, responses, and consequences*. Routledge.

Chapter 4
Artistic Expression in Game Design

Abstract This chapter addresses the debate on whether video games can be considered art by shifting attention from primarily philosophical and institutional arguments to the perspectives of game design professionals. After outlining key moments in the cultural and legal legitimation of video games, alongside contrasting scholarly positions, the chapter identifies a persistent gap in existing research: the limited inclusion of designers' everyday viewpoints in discussions of game aesthetics and artistic value. Using Grounded Theory analysis of semi-structured interviews, the chapter develops an empirically grounded conceptual model centred on the core category "Unveiling When Video Game is Art." Findings indicate that designers do not regard video games as inherently artistic in all cases; rather, artistic status is understood as conditional. The model distinguishes between why a video game may be art, through artistic features (e.g., creativity, storytelling, the integration of technological and artistic languages, and player expression) and artistic effects (e.g., emotional impact, reflection, escapism, and learning), and how art is embodied in games, both through specific components (e.g., graphic style, soundtrack, mechanics, interface) and through the medium's distinctive properties, especially collectivity and interactivity.

4.1 Introduction: Addressing Aesthetics in Digital Games

The acknowledgment of an artistic value within video games has been at the centre of a vivid debate involving researchers and intellectuals from multiple perspectives for decades. Such a discourse centres around questioning whether it is reasonable to recognise video games as a contemporary art form, and, additionally, identifying the possible reasons to motivate such proposition. The roots of such reflections can be traced in institutional and normative initiatives that framed video games as an art form, accounting for their artistic nature (Dannenberg & Davenport, 2018; Parker, 2013). Ever since the late 1980s, museums have opened their doors to video games as cultural artefacts to be exhibited, redefining the aesthetic boundaries of video games. Between 1989 and 1990, the Museum of the Moving Image hosted

M. Mengoni et al., *Digital Game Design*, https://doi.org/10.1007/978-3-032-23320-2_4

an exhibition of video arcade games including game classics like *Space Invaders* and *Pac-Man*, receiving mixed reaction from the audience (Wolf, 2001). Through that exhibition, the Museum was recognising video games as a medium that stands at the end of a trajectory first drawn by television and film. Other cultural institutions embraced this mission in the subsequent years. Walker Art Center's 1998 "Beyond Interface", San Francisco MoMA's 2001 "010101—Art in Technological Times", Whitney Museum's 2001 "BitStreams" or Barbican's Centre 2002 "Game On" are all examples of early exhibitions that challenge and redesign the paradigms of contemporary art, associating video games to digital art (Holmes, 2002; Stalker, 2005). Between 2012 and 2022, the Museum of Modern Art (MoMA) acquired up to 36 video games to be part of a new category of artworks in the exhibition "Never Alone", including vintage and contemporary games like *Pac-Man, Tetris, The Sims, flOw* and *Passage* (Antonelli & Galloway, 2022). Differently from other contemporary experiences, such as the Grand Palais's "Game History" (2012), the Smithsonian American Art Museum's "The Art of Video Games" (2012), or the Victoria and Albert Musem's 2018 "Videogames: Design/Play/Disrupt", the MoMA established a permanent collection dedicated to video games, marking a significant moment in the journey of video games within high culture circuits. In this direction, Berlin's Computerspielemuseum is entirely dedicated to video games. Such experiences were contrasting a widespread resistance to the idea of video games as art, stigmatising it as forms of subculture or merely commercial products. More recently, the game designer Jason Rohrer was the protagonist of an exhibition at Davis Museum, titled "The Game Worlds of Jason Rohrer" (2016). The exhibitions not only celebrates video game products as art products, but also recognises the status of artist to a single game designer, marking a significant milestone in the recognition of artistry in video game design through a novel form of legitimation. Parallel to the establishment of an institutional framing of video games within the realm of interactive art or digital art, international regulations paved the way to further legitimate video games as forms of artistic expression in terms of legal status. The World Intellectual Property Organisation (WIPO) recognises the protection of video games by copyright by recalling article 2 of the Berne Convention for the Protection of Literary and Artistic Works, placing them at the same level of literature, cinematography or painting. In the same direction, research shows how the American jurisprudence increasingly recognised the importance of intellectual property protections on video games (Dannenberg & Davenport, 2018), even though legal patterns cannot be deemed sufficient to validate them as art (Parker, 2013). Additionally, intellectuals and researchers started speculating on the relationship between video games and art. The idea of video games as examples of interaction design art (as in MoMA's "Never Alone") (Lucas, 2023) resembles philosophers' reflections on contemporary art as a matter of experiences rather than artefacts, generating aesthetic effects in the most diverse modalities and embodiments—as if it acquired an *état gazeux*[1] (Benjamin, 2008; Michaud, 2004). The contemplation of a "communication realm" in contemporary art, where the artistic value is connected to the effects and resonance of an artwork, as well as the continuous expansion of the borders of artisticness (Heinich, 2014), are in line with considerations on video games as (not so) novel forms of art (Folkerts, 2010; Pearce,

2006). Indeed, if the rarefaction of art beyond its physical embodiment (as described by Michaud) led to recognition of a significant complexity within aesthetics consideration, it also opened the doors for new media to become part of this multitude of artistic phenomena (Heinich, 2014). If considerations on video games' cultural impact, legal status and features would allow interpreting them as an emerging art for some researchers (Bourgonjon et al. 2017; Holmes, 2002; Smuts, 2005), video games are still denied art-world prestige as experts failed to reach consensus on the relationship between video games and art. Consequently, the question of *whether* a video game is a work of art and, in that case, *when* it can be such—which calls forth philosophical boundaries but is intrinsically grounded in game design studies—is still unanswered and controversial. Existing studies on the topic, although providing useful insights on this ambiguous scenario, appear to speculate on conceptual levels only, excluding everyday practices from their research picture. The lack of consideration of designers' perspectives might leave a significant gap in the understanding of the dynamics, approaches and features that would support the consideration of video game design as artistic and creative expression. Indeed, a structured mapping of perspectives from game design practitioners could highlight relevant issues and significant trajectories to guide the reflection on game as art. In this blurred variety of positions and interpretations, this chapter aims at identifying whether game designers define their products as works of art or not, and, if they do, defining what are the arguments they use to support such propositions.

Taking part in one of the most contemporary debates, many theorists and scholars have discussed whether video games can be recognised as a legitimate art form with a critical sensitivity. To address this issue, they framed it within an academic perspective, trying to build a scientific reflection upon it. Undoubtedly, a growing body of studies on this topic seems to ascribe artistic potential to video games, specifically acknowledging their unique qualities that set them apart from traditional art forms.

A first line of research recognised video games' artistic potential based on the way they embody interplay between creation and engagement, similar to the dynamic processes observed in a game so ancient as chess, as celebrated by Marcel Duchamp (Molderings, 2010; Pearce, 2006). Duchamp's recognition of the conceptual nature and the nearly infinite possibilities within chess reflects the artistic values inherent in game design, where the designer's craft lies in balancing parameters such as goals, obstacles, and player freedom to create meaningful experiences (Molderings, 2010). Pearce (2006) extended this perspective by asserting that game design, whether it is aimed to produce art games or commercial products, involves a sophisticated understanding of these dynamics to either adhere to or subvert them. This seems to echo Duchamp's view on the act of playing chess, which can be considered as creatively demanding as making art itself. Furthermore, the engagement required in game art, where the artist invites the player to become a co-creator, challenges traditional notions of the art object and its passive consumption (Vorderer & Bryant, 2012). In this line, the dynamic, interactive nature of games as art recalls Duchamp's desire to capture the mental and social dynamics of chess in his works, emphasising the fluid, participatory experience over static observation.

More sustained positions on video games as a legitimate art come from scholars such as Jenkins (2005) and Gee (2006), who were among the first to acknowledge the potential of video games as art within academic discourse. Jenkins (2005) asserted that video games represent a vibrant new art form, "one as appropriate for the digital age as those earlier media were for the machine age" (p. 177). He emphasised that video games offer unique aesthetic experiences and transform computer screens into accessible realms of experimentation and innovation, garnering public interest that other digital art forms have failed to achieve. Similarly, Gee (2006) highlighted the necessity of developing new interpretative frameworks to appreciate the distinct artistic nature of video games. He argued that traditional analytical tools used for literature and film are inadequate for this medium, positing that video games challenge scholars to create new inquiry methodologies.

Smuts (2005) went a step further by trying to offer multiple lenses through which this issue can be framed (e.g., historical, aesthetic, expressive). Specifically, he argued that video games, like traditional artistic forms, have the capacity to evoke deep emotional responses, convey complex narratives, and provide immersive aesthetic experiences. Moreover, in addition to traditional art forms, the interactive nature of video games uniquely enhances their artistic value, as players engage with the medium in a participatory manner, influencing the unfolding of the narrative and the aesthetic experience. In this context, it appears that it is precisely *interactivity* that represents the key feature that sets video games apart from other art forms (Tavinor, 2023; Wolf, 2010). In his theory on digital artworks, the philosopher of art Dominic McIver Lopes (2001) defined games as *strongly interactive* media "because their users' inputs help determine the subsequent state of play" (p. 68). Indeed, he distinguished *strongly interactive* media, in which "the structure itself is shaped in part by the interactor's choices" (p. 68), from *weakly interactive* media, in which the user merely influences the sequence or selection of pre-existing structures. This distinction is crucial for understanding the nature of video games, as they require players to make decisions that directly influence the game's evolving state, actively shaping the potential structures and outcomes of the game.

In a later study, Lopes (2009) also attempted to define several *qualities of art* characterising games. He asserted that they not only can possess aesthetic qualities, but can also express emotions and be intellectually stimulating. They can also exhibit formal complexity, as they can convey intricate meanings and reflect individual viewpoints, requiring substantial creative imagination and skill in their creation. However, some of the characteristics traditionally attributed to art (e.g., originality or conformity to established artistic forms) may not suit the area of video games.

Besides Lopes (2009), other researchers gradually contributed to the enrichment of the academic debate on video games as an art form, offering various standpoints on *why* videogames can be art and *how* they can induce an artistic experience (Adams, 2006; Bourgonjon et al., 2017; Folkerts, 2010).

In exploring the potential of video games to be recognised as an art form, Adams (2006) posited several critical considerations. He argued that for games to attain artistic status, they must transcend mere entertainment and embrace broader aesthetic and narrative ambitions akin to other established art forms like film and literature. In addition, they must also challenge players intellectually and emotionally, similarly to how great artworks challenge viewers, fostering new perspectives and understandings. Similar concepts were then traced by Folkerts (2010), according to whom video games can be regarded as a form of art due to their capacity to generate meaning through narrative and interactive play. Indeed, Folkerts sees the artistic nature of games as rooted not in their visual aesthetics but in their ability to engage players in second-order representations, which involve a deeper cognitive and emotional engagement with the game's narrative and mechanics (2010). This engagement leads to metacognitive reflection, where players contemplate their in-game decisions and their broader implications, mirroring the introspective experiences often elicited by traditional art forms. Accordingly, by projecting their values and desires onto virtual characters, players undergo a reflective and potentially transformative experience, underscoring the notion that games, like other art forms, can provoke profound personal and cultural insights.

However, novelty often has a hard time being accepted, especially when it comes to art, just as there has been in photography or cinema (Martin, 2007). The main contrarian position in the literature against the recognition of videogames as art is represented by Ebert (2010), who ascribed to the intrinsic features of videogames their disqualification from being genuine art forms. He saw the competitive and interactive nature of videogames as opposed to the qualities of traditional art forms such as literature, film, and theatre, where audience members are passive recipients of an artist's controlled narrative. Indeed, he asserted that videogames, being defined by rules, objectives, and the possibility of winning, fundamentally differ from the experiential nature of serious art. Additionally, he noted the absence of a game masterpiece comparable to achievements of great poets, novelists, and filmmakers, suggesting this further undermines the artistic credibility of videogames.

Nevertheless, Ebert seems to be one of the few who expressed such a strong contrary position. It is more common indeed to find more neutral and/or positive perspectives on the consideration of videogames as art. Bourgonjon et al. (2017), for instance, presented an overview of viewpoints on their artistic status, rather than providing a definitive answer on the matter. The authors mapped three main perspectives on video games as art: (1) they connected video games with historical definitions of art; (2) they advocated for a functional approach, emphasising how video games facilitate creative expression and impact audiences; (3) they argued for a close examination of the social impact of video games and their potential to influence society. Jagoda (2017) instead stated that videogames "are not a uniform and coherent contemporary form but, as a mass medium, they manifest a form of sociopolitical intervention, an element of everyday life, a form of personal expression, and a medium for artistic production" (p. 213). Therefore, despite rejecting the definition of videogames as an 'art form', he still acknowledges their expressive capacity, rooted in the artistic connotation of the medium.

More recently, taking one step further, the philosopher of the arts and academic Tavinor (2023) wondered whether video games are works of art or an art form[2]. To address this contentious issue, he attempted to offer a more systematic view on it, shedding light on the complexity and the multi-faceted nature of this debate. Specifically, the author distinguished between the mere presence of artistic design in games and their recognition as artworks, arguing that not all video games need to be art to validate the medium as an art form. Indeed, he refuted Ebert's (2010) 'masterpiece argument' by noting that a medium's lack of universal acclaim does not preclude it from being art. Additionally, Tavinor advocated for a "cluster theory" approach, suggesting that games such as *Skyrim* exhibit many of the characteristics associated with art, including aesthetic properties, creativity, and formal complexity. Therefore, while not all video games may qualify as art, he affirmed that the medium as a whole has the potential to be recognised as an art form.

Despite video games' cultural significance and the growing body of research acknowledging their potential artistic status (Adams, 2006; Bourgonjon et al., 2017; Folkerts, 2010; Gee, 2006; Jenkins, 2005; Lopes, 2001, 2010; Pearce, 2006; Smuts, 2005), there does not seem to be a conclusive model that indicates a shared perspective on the debate of video games as art. Additionally, while existing studies contribute with conceptual insights, they tend to be mainly theoretical, neglecting the practical viewpoints of game designers, whose perspectives could enrich the discussion of the artistic dimensions of game creation and innovation. Therefore, looking at this issue from the designers' perspective could provide the key to explore and interpret the dynamics and characteristics behind video games as a form of creative expression and artistic endeavour.

4.1.1 When Video Game is Art

This section illustrates the results of the qualitative analysis of the interviews conducted with the game designers. The categories and codes identified and presented in the following subparagraphs unveil how game designers tend to acknowledge how video games are not always necessarily a form of art, but rather respond to a set of conditions which, if present, determine their artistic value. In this sense, game designers unveiled *why* video game can be art (e.g., the features that assign artistic value to a video game), and, when it is, *how* video game is art (e.g., the dimensions that characterise video games as art). As a result, the Grounded Theory analysis of designers' perspectives led to the definition of the Core Category "Unveiling When Video Game is Art". The model is composed of two distinct categories: *Why Video Game is Art* and *How Video Game is Art*: such categories, combined together, can provide designers' overall view on the relationship between video games and art. As the first category sets the preliminary conditions to which such a discourse could be established, defining the features and effects of video games that can be defined as "artistic", the second category identifies the specific characteristics of such an art medium. In this sense, the conditions for the recognition of an artistic value (*Why Video Game is Art*) create the conceptual basis that allows a reflection upon video games as art (*How Video Game is Art*). The two categories complementarily specify the main trajectories through which art is embodied in video games. Figure 4.1

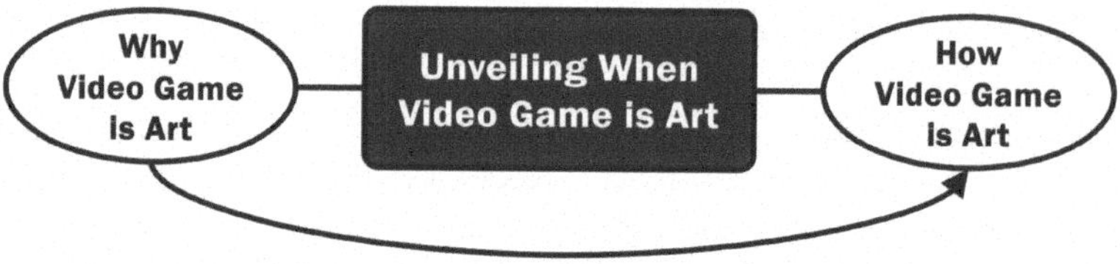

Fig. 4.1 Conceptual model of designers' perspectives on video games as art. The model consists of two main categories, "Why Video Game is Art" and "How Video Game is Art," which together form the core category "Unveiling When Video Game is Art"

shows the graphic presentation of the conceptual model. The Core Category, which is posed in the middle of the figure, is connected to both categories, as they concurrently contribute to its definition. Additionally, an arrow connects the *Why* category to the *How* category, underlining how the second one logically depends on the former one.

4.1.2 Core Category: Unveiling When Video Game is Art

Designers' reflections upon the artistic value of video games centre around a primary consideration: video games *can* be art, but they do not necessarily achieve this status under any condition. This central proposition led designers to the logical need to identify the circumstances under which it is possible to affirm that a video game is art. In this sense, game designers identified the reasons why it is legitimate to envision the potential of art in video games. As game designers identified such circumstances, they were also able to define video games as an artistic medium, specifying the characteristics that distinguish it from other art forms and therefore positioning video games among the arts acknowledging their unique features. In this sense, game designers undertook an interpretational step that leads their discourse towards an etiological level (i.e., causative considerations). The *Why* category informs the *How* category in the sense that, without identifying the artistic features of video games, a discourse on video games as art in its specificities would be unfounded. When combining the reasons why video games can be associated with art and the ways through which art can be uniquely embodied in video games, the core category emerges: in this sense, game designers are defining the boundaries of video games as art on the whole (i.e., when video games are art, fulfilling specific conditions and possessing specific features).

4.1.3 Why Video Game is Art

The first key aspect that emerged from the interviews is connected to the definition of the reasons why it would be considered appropriate to associate video games to art. In this sense, designers undertook an interpretational step to critically reflect upon the relationship between art and video games, sharing their thoughts and opinions with reference to the aspects that can qualify video games as art and that play a crucial role in determining its artistic value. *Why Video Game is Art* is composed of two sub-categories: *Artistic Features* and *Artistic Effects*, respectively highlighting the elements of video games that are proper of art according to common sense and the reactions or effects that they can generate (See Table 4.1).

Artistic Features

With reference to the first dimension, Artistic Features, four codes were identified from the analysis of interviewees' perspectives. The first artistic feature that was highlighted consists in associating video games to any other piece of art, considering how it is the product of a creative process (Video games are a product of creativity, n = 2). The capacity of video games to narrate a story was identified as the second artistic feature (Video games can narrate a story, n = 3). The other two aspects interpreted as artistic features are the combination of technology and artistic languages in video games (Video games combine technology and artistic language, n = 4) and, lastly, video games' potential to give users freedom of expression (Video games give users freedom of expression, n = 8).

Artistic Effects

This sub-category encompasses what interviewees identified as outcomes of the experience with video games that can be associated with the sensations and effects of the fruition of art. In this sense, video games are considered to be art because, as any other piece of art, they can generate a feeling of escapism and illusion of being present in another dimension (Video games can generate escapism, n = 1), they can stimulate a reflection upon specific themes or topics they deal with (Video games can stimulate reflection, n = 3), they can evoke positive or negative emotions (such as gratification, joy, disgust, fear, anxiety, and so on) (Video games can evoke emotions, n = 8) and, lastly, they can trigger learning, prompting the transmission of knowledge and information (Video games can trigger learning, n = 1). Taking a look at codes' incidence, the interpretation of video games as art based on their potential to generate emotions is the most diffused consideration made by interviewees.

4.1.4 How Video Game is Art

The second dimension emerging from designers' narratives refers to the features that characterise video games as art and distinguish them from other art forms. As these

Table 4.1 Why video game is art

Sub-category	Code	Sentences	Number of participants
Artistic features	Video games are a product of creativity	"It's the result of the artistic expression of what's inside of us." (P1)	2 (18%)
	Video games can narrate a story	"There are many video games in which the story and its narration could easily hold a candle to the deepest piece of avant garde cinema." (P11)	3 (27%)
	Video games combine technology and artistic language	"It's obviously art as it mixes two very complex dimensions: tech and artistic expression." (P4)	4 (36%)
	Video games give users freedom of expression	"There are video games that give you incredible opportunities for self-expression and that's art too: letting the player express their abilities." (P5)	8 (73%)
Artistic effects	Video games can generate escapism	"Video games are a form of art even only for the fact that […] they allow a moment of pause, stop the natural affliction of human beings." (P10)	1 (9%)
	Video games can stimulate reflection	"What defines a game as a work of art is the experience that it takes you to […]. A game can touch upon topics related to what it is to experience love, tragedy or existential questions in terms of what is the purpose of all this […] going into a more philosophical pattern." (P6)	3 (27%)
	Video games can evoke emotions	"There are feelings that a game can evoke and no other medium can." (P9)	8 (73%)
	Video games can trigger learning	"You have to wrap it up carefully, you can place it as something intellectual because people are afraid of culture, but at the end of the experience they played an extremely cultural game and they learnt something." (P10)	1 (9%)

reflections are completely descriptive, they represent attempts to provide a definition of video game art, identifying characterising elements and relevant features. To this end, two main levels can be assessed in the analysis of interviewees' perspectives (see Table 4.2). The first sub-category, *Art in Video Game Parts*, unveils each specific aspect that could be considered as artistic by itself. The aspects highlighted by game designers are four (constituting, respectively, the sub-category's four codes): *Graphic Style* (n = 4), *Soundtrack* (n = 1), *Game mechanics* (n = 2) and *User Interface* (n = 2). Such elements were identified as potential standalone contributors to the artistic value of video games. When looking at the number of participants that mentioned the codes, the prevalence of graphic style as an artistic element of video games emerges with clearance.

Table 4.2 How Video Game is Art

Sub-category	Code	Sentences	Number of participants
Art in video game parts	Graphic style	"I knew I wanted to welcome the player and then disturb them, so I chose a warm colour palette because I wanted to create the aesthetic feeling of warmth […]. I wanted a game that was soft in its colours, in its shapes." (P10)	4 (36%)
	Soundtrack	"What would a game be without a soundtrack? Our composer is a genius and does things that excite the studio." (P2)	1 (9%)
	Game mechanics	"I can tell you about the programmer who, as we were saying before, does the insane mechanics, and for me that's also a work of art." (P7)	2 (18%)
	User interface	"To this end, the attention for UI is also fundamental both in the ideation and the development phases." (P11)	2 (18%)
Art as a whole	Video game as collective art	"It's the result of the artistic expression of what we all have inside. The moment you express something you have inside, your creativity… that is art." (P1)	3 (27%)
	Video game as interactive art	"It's the only interactive media that we have: if you're reading a book or watching a movie you can only project yourself towards a character, but at the end of the day […] is the character from (the book or) the movie that made the decision […]. Whereas in a game it's not a projection, that choice is in front of you." (P6)	8 (73%)

The second sub-category, *Art as a Whole*, adopts a wider perspective, looking at the specific features of video games as an artistic medium from a holistic perspective. In this line, two main properties were underlined by interviewees (see Table 4.2). On the production side, video games were defined as a *collective* artistic language, deriving from the combined contributions of multiple creative professionals (*Video game as collective art,* $n = 3$). On the fruition side, video games were defined as an *interactive* artistic language, involving the user through multiple degrees of freedom of initiative and allowing them to actively take part in the work of art, co-determining and co-creating their experience (*Video game as interactive art,* $n = 8$). With reference to the incidence of the two codes, the interactive dimension was mentioned more often than the collective one.

4.1.5 Discussion

When looking at the main results from this Grounded Theory analysis, it is interesting to note that, following Tavinor's masterpiece argument (2023), participants' insights can be positioned in the 'artwork perspective'. Consequently, the fact that some video games can be considered as pieces of art does not necessarily mean that every video game is intrinsically art (i.e., 'art form perspective'). This result shows a substantial distance between participants' perspectives and literature advocating for video games to be recognised as an art form (Gee, 2006; Jenkins, 2005; Smuts, 2005; Tavinor, 2023). However, interviewees recognised the artistic potential of this medium. The framework deriving from the Grounded Theory analysis of game designers' perspective on the aesthetic value of video games centres around the identification of necessary conditions, essential features and core motivations to qualify video games as art. Accordingly, participants disclosed not only the elements that play a fundamental role in determining the potential artistic essence of video games, but also the lines of reasoning underlying such perspectives.

When interviewees were asked about the connection between video games and art, they mentioned a series of aspects and effects that they consider to be 'artistic'. Such inputs do resonate with scientific literature, as illustrated below.

The code "Video games are a product of creativity" appeared explicitly in only two interviews. However, it is important to note that, when looking at the whole body of codes developed, it appears that the process of game design is intended by interviewees as a creative process that sees the contribution of multiple professionals with their ideas and stimuli (Cormio et al., 2024).

One of the dimensions that was highlighted among the artistic features of video games is their ability to narrate a story. With reference to the dimension of storytelling, art has always been recognised as a means through which stories can be narrated across cultures and time periods (Jain, 2021). Accordingly, literature recognises the narrative potential of video games, often embedding processes of sense-making and empathy, stimulating reflections on values and ideas (Barab et al., 2010). This echoes Adams' correlation of video games' narrative features with other art forms (2006), as well as Folkerts's claims about video games' potential to generate meaning through embedded narrative elements (2010). In this sense, the elements of immersion and interactivity (which are present in different degrees depending on the game itself) can augment the power of narration and the control over it by the user, as highlighted by participants. In this same perspective, the code "Video games give users freedom of expression" opens up reflections on player experience and freedom of choice. Pointing towards the feature of interactivity, the opportunity given to users to navigate the video game dimension with different levels of exploratory freedom distinguishes video games from most art forms (Folkerts, 2010; Toh & Kirschner, 2020). The stress on interactivity and user freedom manifested by interviewees appears to be in line with Molderings' reflections upon the nature of game design (2010). This understanding of video game experience is also connected to their potential educational value in light of the opportunity to experiment solutions and practice decision-making in a controlled setting (Dishon, 2021). In the realm of art, participants seem to hint that video games could be aligned with the branch of *interactive art*, that aims at involving the spectator in different modalities to produce meaning and finds its apex in electronic and digital art forms (Molderings, 2010; Muller et al., 2006; Soler-Adillon, 2015). The code "Video games combine technology and artistic language" appears to highlight the multitude of media that are embedded in video games and that are situated between hardware-software features and creative expression, as hinted by Heinich (2014). It is not unusual that literature recognises in digital games a relationship between technological elements and aesthetics effects, seeing elements such as mechanics, sound or graphics typically intertwined with aesthetic experience (Niedenthal, 2009).

When considering the artistic effects of video games, interviewees' narrations appear to highlight four interconnected experiences: escapism, reflection, emotional connection and learning. With reference to the dimension of escapism, art is interpreted as a means of liberation from everyday life and social obligations (Marcuse, 2006). Interviewees underlined how specific features of video games give the dimension of escapism a more complex turn compared to other art forms, considering how digital games are often perceived as inherently escapist due to their virtuality and their recreational use, allowing gamers to 'escape real life', as confirmed by related studies (Calleja, 2010). Correlated to the artistic features of storytelling and freedom of choice, video games were recognised by interviewees as means through which reflection can be stimulated. In this sense, participants underlined how video games constitute a space in which users can critically reflect upon specific topics (Gandhi et al., 2022; Rüth & Kaspar, 2021). Such a perspective echoes Lopes's idea of intellectual and emotional stimulation (2010), as well as Adams's considerations on what could make a video game akin to any other powerful artwork (2006). Participants connected the dimension of reflection with emotions and empathy, as well as learning processes, which scientific literature recognises as well (Barab et al., 2010). Participants underlined the relationship between players' engagement, interactivity and immersion (recalling the concept of escapism), illustrating how it can foster emotional experiences through different means (e.g., choice, flow, avatar customisation, game plot), overcoming the mere scope of entertainment. Such views are confirmed by research on the topic (Callejas-Cuervo et al., 2017; Isbister, 2017). With regards to learning, scientific literature shows how video games can be a powerful tool for situated and dynamic learning at multiple levels, offering opportunities for experiencing situations and phenomena in controlled gamified settings (Cole et al., 2024; Martinez et al., 2022; Toh & Kirschner, 2020). However, only one out of all participants mentioned learning as an artistic effect, relating it to what could happen when seeing a painting or listening to a piece of classical music. In general, interviewees' insights could suggest how the potential of art (and, therefore, video games) to trigger transformative experiences depends on the modalities through which it is experienced.

The analysis of designers' perspectives revealed also a second dimension that explains how video game is art. Such a dimension manifests itself in a dual characterisation of video games creation: *Art in Video Game Parts* and *Art as a Whole.*

With reference to the first one, interviewees shed light on the role played by single video games parts, such as graphic style, soundtrack, game mechanics, and user interface, which may appear secondary when looking at the artistry of a video game, but may turn out to be relevant details for game designers in the construction of an artistic value. These parts of video games seem to fall under what some academics (Adams, 2006; Lopes, 2010) have identified as the 'aesthetic qualities' of a game. For instance, in discussing the importance of video games having an aesthetic, Adams (2006) referred generically to the possible existence of multiple aesthetics of a game: drawing a parallel with the film world, he compared, for example, the "seamlessness of the experience" of a game to the editing of a film (p. 261). The philosopher Lopes (2010) also acknowledged the coexistence of various aesthetic qualities, but highlighted how, differently from traditional art forms, video games interactivity allows them to realise aesthetic properties in a unique way, yet without specifying what these properties are. It is interesting to note that the interviewees, with their practical point of view and daily exposure to the flourishing video game industry, seem to have given concrete form to what have been generically referred to as 'aesthetic qualities'. Visual elements such as colour, mood or tone can be impactful when designing the game *user interface* or when creating a certain *graphic style.* The use of colour can play an important role in creating a certain experience or atmosphere, for example by intervening on contrast, light or tone, and also affecting emotions and feelings (Goethe, 2019). For instance, one of the interviewees emphasised how the visual aspect can support what one wants to convey to the player, stating how the choice of the colour palette influences the emotional state of the player. Another essential artistic part mentioned by interviewees is the soundtrack. The use of music in video games can underpin and foster players' perception of the gameworld, their involvement, but also the game narrative (Munday, 2007). This concept was underlined by one interviewee, who stated the central role that soundtracks play in the design of a video game. Finally, the last important piece that was mentioned is represented by game mechanics, which contribute, together with other elements such as graphics or sound, to the construction of the formal meaning of game (Folkerts, 2010; Niedenthal, 2009). The fact that the interviewees considered game mechanics as one of the game parts in which art can be embodied is certainly something that catches the eye. The MDA framework considers mechanics as one of the three essential parts in the game design process, alongside dynamics an aesthetics (Hunicke et al., 2004), defining it as "the various actions, behaviours, and control mechanisms afforded to the player within a game context" (Kim, 2015, p.18). However, designers' quite remarkably appeared to consider game mechanics as a further factor that contributes to the game aesthetics, rather than a counterpart part of it. Indeed, game mechanics were considered art themselves by some interviewees. It is also remarkable how elements such as graphic style, user interface or soundtrack, together with other aesthetic features such as narrative, can contribute in generating an artistic value so that "all elements of the game work together in harmony without any false notes" (Adams, 2006, p. 261). The prevailing dimension from which this aspect emerged seems to be graphics, emphasising the primacy of the visual aesthetics when considering the artistic value of video games, despite the multitude of languages they offer, diverging from Folkerts's idea that the artistic nature of games is not rooted in their visual aesthetics. Designers underlined how graphics can be linked for example to the soundtrack, as these two elements can creatively influence each other, but can also produce an aesthetic effect, evoking emotion in the player. However, the visual aspects alone are not enough to be considered art, as rightly recalled by P6, who affirmed: "Beauty is not the only thing you need in order to have art. Art can be ugly but it evokes an emotion. So aesthetically alone I do not think that a game could be considered as an art piece".

These are only a few examples showing how artistic parts of video games are varied, equally important, and can naturally intertwine with artistic features and effects (Smuts, 2005), such as the ability to stimulate the intellect, evoke emotions and narrate a story, and it is precisely this coexistence that strengthens the expressive power of a game.

The second dimension that explains how video game is art, *Art as a Whole*, is embodied in a two-fold nature of video games: "Video game as collective art" and "Video game as interactive art".

With reference to the first, game designers reflected on the importance of the collective dimension when creating video games, as everyone can bring their own unique creative perspective. Specifically, interviewees underlined how the collective, creative expression of each group member appears as a powerful tool for corroborating the artistic value of the final digital product, as long as all team members work together towards a common vision and bring their own personality, taking care not to run the risk of tunnel vision. Indeed, although video games allow for the reflection of individual viewpoints (Lopes, 2010), it is essential for team members to avoid over-focusing on their specific areas of interest, as this can potentially lead to the loss of the overall vision of the project, as reported in a previous study (Cormio et al., 2024). Additionally, designers highlighted how essential communication among team members, learning from each other, and sharing a common vision could be useful to achieve an effective collaboration (Tran & Biddle, 2008).

The other representative nature of *Art as Whole* is the shared consideration of games as interactive art. As stated by the majority of the interviewees, interactivity seems to be the key characteristic representing the nature of video games and distinguishing such an artistic media from traditional art forms (Tavinor, 2023; Wolf, 2010). Specifically, participants underlined how players are given the opportunity to be actively protagonists of their experience, extending the mere identification with a character that takes place when reading a book or watching a movie. Indeed, the game designers' narrative confirmed the belief, already established in the literature, that interactivity is inherent in video games, as it is the players' choices that influence their outcome, rather than offering predetermined ones (Vorderer & Bryant, 2012). Video games still possess the capacities of traditional art forms (e.g., evoke emotions or exhibit a narrative potential), but in addition they uniquely engage 'spectators' in a participatory way (Smuts, 2005), being what Lopes (2001) interestingly defined as "strongly interactive media" (p. 68), where users' inputs influence the evolving state of play, creating a fluid ad adaptive experience. The engagement in game design thus mirrors Duchamp's artistic vision, as the player's role as co-creator challenges traditional notions of art as a passive experience, further emphasising the artistic value of interactivity underscored by game designers (Molderings, 2010; Pearce, 2006).

4.1.5.1 Implications: Making Art and Crafting Games

The aim of this chapter was to understand if video game design can be recognised as a form of artistic practice through the identification of game designers' perspectives, insights and experiences. To this end, the chapter proposed an investigation of game designers' perceptions and attitudes on the relationship between video games and art. The framework, developed through the application of the three-step coding method of Grounded Theory, brings together all the insights that were collected through the interviews, deriving a shared perspective on the debate of video games artistic potential based on designers' experience. The bottom-up qualitative approach allowed a deeper understanding of video games as art acknowledging the voice of game designers, enriching the reflections on such themes by providing experience-based knowledge and contributions. As scholars from different disciplinary areas ventured into studying the relationship between game and art, the perspective of game design practitioners allowed us to highlight relevant topics and significant dimensions in a multitude of scientific positions and interpretations.

The conceptual framework that was developed centres around the core category *Unveiling When Video Game is Art*, which is composed of two distinct categories: *Why Video Game is Art* and *How Video Game is Art*. As highlighted from the interviews, game designers do acknowledge that video games, although not always necessarily representing a form of art, can possess artistic value in specific conditions. In the first place, according to interviewees, video games can present a set of features, such as storytelling, and provide users with specific effects that designers associate to art, such as stimulating reflections or evoking emotions (*Why Video Game is Art*). In the second place, game designers underlined how, when video games can be considered as art, their artistic value can be embedded in specific components (e.g., graphic style or soundtrack), and, as an artistic language, they present specific features that distinguish it from any other (e.g., interactivity features) (*How Video Game is Art*). Consequently, all the reflections on how video games can be art are primarily based on the effective possibility to define them as art (i.e., why they are art). As a result, game designers' insights appear to belong to the 'artwork perspective' (Tavinor, 2023), but do reflect multiple findings coming from scientific literature in a combined, organic and original perspective.

The research illustrated in this chapter presents multiple limitations. Firstly, researchers did not provide game designers with a specific definition of the concepts of 'art' or 'art form', nor did they ask game designers what they mean with such expressions when using them. In this sense, this study combined perspectives that might also derive from different conceptualisations and interpretations of what art is. However, as the chapter aims at reflecting on experience-based perspectives on game design, its results can still be found insightful. An indication of the experience-based nature of this research lies in the low percentage of the frequency of certain codes, which is indicative of the strong subjectiveness of the topic. The present study can be considered as a first attempt to deepen the knowledge on the relationship between video games and art based on designers' experiences. Such an effort could be followed by further assessments on a larger scale to test the reliability of the developed conceptual framework, the generalisability of these results and possible differences based on game designers' cultural and professional backgrounds. In this direction, further investigations could provide insights to integrate and optimise the conceptual framework. Additionally, an investigation on users' perceptions on video games as an art form could provide a significant point of view to address this discourse. Given its limitations, this research can still represent a contribution to the discourse on the relationship between video games and art, providing a theoretical comprehensive framework that is based on the everyday experiences of professionals belonging to this field.

Notes

1. The concept of art in an "état gazeux" was introduced by the philosopher Yves Michaud in his work titled "L'art à l'état gazeux. Essai sur le triomphe de l'esthétique" (2003) and refers to the paradoxical contemporary condition of art and beauty. As the latter has spread across all contexts of human life (through the pursuit and cult of aesthetics, from emotional and spiritual wellbeing to tourism and fashion), there is an essential lack of traditional works of art, requiring the redefinition of boundaries between what would be considered as art and what would not.
2. He interestingly wrote: "though Duchamp's Fountain (1917) is an artwork, urinals themselves are not an art form in virtue of this fact. Duchamp merely repurposed the urinal to create art" (p. 82).

References

Adams, E. W. (2006). Will computer games ever be a legitimate art form? *Journal of Media Practice, 7*(1), 67–77.

Antonelli, P., & Galloway, P. (2022). When video games came to the museum. *MoMA online magazine*. Retrieved from: https://www.moma.org/magazine/articles/798.

Barab, S. A., Dodge, T., Ingram-Goble, A., Volk, C., Peppler, K. A., Pettyjohn, P., & Solomou, M. (2010). Pedagogical dramas and transformational play: Narratively rich games for learning. *Mind, Culture, and Activity, 17*(3), 235–264.

Benjamin, W. (2008). *The work of art in the age of mechanical reproduction* (J. A. Underwood, Trans.). Penguin Books. (Original work published 1935).

Berne Convention for the Protection of Literary and Artistic Works, September 9, 1886, revised at Paris July 24, 1971. Retrieved from: https://www.law.cornell.edu/treaties/berne/overview.html#2.

Bourgonjon, J., Vandermeersche, G., Rutten, K., & Quinten, N. (2017). Perspectives on video games as art. *CLCWeb: Comparative Literature and Culture, 19*(4), 1.

Calleja, G. (2010). Digital games and escapism. *Games and Culture, 5*(4), 335–353.
Callejas-Cuervo, M., Martínez-Tejada, L. A., & Alarcón-Aldana, A. C. (2017). Emotion recognition techniques using physiological signals and video games—Systematic review. *Revista Facultad De Ingenieria-Universidad De Antioquia, 26*, 19–28.
Charmaz, K. (2014). *Constructing grounded theory*. Sage.
Cole, C., Parada, R. H., & Mackenzie, E. (2024). A scoping review of video games and learning in secondary classrooms. *Journal of Research on Technology in Education, 56*(5), 544–577.
Corbin, J. M., & Strauss, A. L. (2015). *Basics of qualitative research: Techniques and procedures for developing grounded theory* (4th ed.). Sage.
Cormio, L., Giaconi, C., Mengoni, M., & Santilli, T. (2024). Exploring game design approaches through conversations with designers. *Design Studies, 91*, Article 101253.
Dannenberg, R., & Davenport, J. (2018). Top 10 video game cases (US): How video game litigation in the US has evolved since the advent of Pong. *Interactive Entertainment Law Review, 1*(2), 89–102.
De Smet, M. M., Meganck, R., Van Nieuwenhove, K., Truijens, F. L., & Desmet, M. (2019). No change? A grounded theory analysis of depressed patients' perspectives on non-improvement in psychotherapy. *Frontiers in Psychology, 10*, 588.
Deleuze, J., Maurage, P., Schimmenti, A., Nuyens, F., Melzer, A., & Billieux, J. (2019). Escaping reality through videogames is linked to an implicit preference for virtual over real-life stimuli. *Journal of Affective Disorders, 245*, 1024–1031.
Dishon, G. (2021). The designability paradox: Rethinking authenticity and situatedness in educational video games. *Educational Technology Research and Development, 69*(2), 497–513.
Ebert, R. (2010). *Games can never be art*. Retrieved from https://www.rogerebert.com/roger-ebert/video-games-can-never-be-art.
Folkerts, J. (2010). Playing games as an art experience: How videogames produce meaning through narrative and play. In *Emerging Practices in Cyberculture and Social Networking* (pp. 97–117). Brill.
Gandhi, K., Miller, J. A., & Cooper, S. (2022). "Philosophy is Seeped into Every Brick"-Weaving Reflective Elements into Mass-Market Games. In *Proceedings of the 17th International Conference on the Foundations of Digital Games* (pp. 1–10).
Gee, J. P. (2006). Why game studies now? Video games: A new art form. *Games and Culture, 1*(1), 58–61.
Goethe, O. (2019). Visual aesthetics in games and gamification. *Gamification Mindset. Human–Computer Interaction Series*, 85–92.
Heinich, N. (2014). *Le paradigme de l'art contemporain: Structures d'une révolution artistique.* Gallimard.
Holmes, T. (2002). *Art games and breakout: New media meets the American arcade*. Retrieved 05/09/2024 from: https://www.crudeoils.us/artwrite/August2002/Holmes.htm.
Hsiao, H. (2007). A brief review of digital games and learning. In *2007 First IEEE International Workshop on Digital Game and Intelligent Toy Enhanced Learning (DIGITEL'07)*, 124–129.
Hull, S. (2013). *Doing grounded theory: Notes for the aspiring qualitative analyst*. University of Cape Town.
Hunicke, R., LeBlanc, M., & Zubek, R. (2004). MDA: A formal approach to game design and game research. In *Proceedings of the AAAI Workshop on Challenges in Game AI* (Vol. 4, No. 1, p. 1722).
Isbister, K. (2017). *How Games Move Us—Emotion by Design*. MIT Press.
Jagoda, P. (2017). Videogame criticism and games in the twenty-first century. *American Literary History, 29*(1), 205–218.
Jain, A. (2021). Role of narration in visual arts from history to contemporary. *International Journal of Applied Research, 3*(8), 877–882.
Jenkins, H. (2005). Games, the new lively art. *Handbook of computer game studies*, 175–189.

Kallio, H., Pietilä, A. M., Johnson, M., & Kangasniemi, M. (2016). Systematic methodological review: Developing a framework for a qualitative semi-structured interview guide. *Journal of Advanced Nursing, 72*(12), 2954–2965.
Kim, B. (2015). Game mechanics, dynamics, and aesthetics. *Library Technology Reports, 51*(2), 17–19.
Klayman, J. (1995). Varieties of confirmation bias. *Psychology of Learning and Motivation, 32*, 385–418.
Lopes, D. M. M. (2001). The ontology of interactive art. *Journal of Aesthetic Education*, 65–81.
Lopes, D. M. (2010). *A philosophy of computer art*. Routledge.
Lucas, J. (2023). The puzzle of putting video games in a museum. *The New Yorker*. Retrieved 05/09/2024 from: https://www.newyorker.com/culture/the-art-world/the-puzzle-of-putting-video-games-in-a-museum.
Marcuse, H. (2006). *Art and liberation: collected papers of Herbert Marcuse, Volume 4*. In D. Kellner (Ed.) (1st ed.). Routledge.
Martin, B. (2007). Should videogames be viewed as art. *Videogames and Art, 2*, 345–356.
Martinez, L., Gimenes, M., & Lambert, E. (2022). Entertainment video games for academic learning: A systematic review. *Journal of Educational Computing Research, 60*(5), 1083–1109.
Michaud, Y. (2004). *L'art à l'état gazeux: Essai sur le triomphe de l'esthétique*. Hachette. (Original work published 2003).
Molderings, H. (2010). *Duchamp and the aesthetics of chance: Art as experiment*. Columbia University Press.
Muller, L, Edmonds, E, & Connel, M. (2006). Living laboratories for interactive art. *CoDesign, 2*(4).
Munday, R. (2007). Music in video games. *Music, sound and multimedia: From the live to the virtual*, 51–67.
Newman, J. (2004). *Videogames* (1st ed.). Routledge.
Niedenthal, S. (2009). What we talk about when we talk about game aesthetics. In *Proceedings of DiGRA 2009 Conference: Breaking New Ground: Innovation in Games, Play, Practice and Theory*.
Parker, J. R. (2013). Games are art: Video games as theatrical performance. *IEEE International Games Innovation Conference (IGIC), 2013*, 203–208.
Pearce, C. (2006). Games as art: The aesthetics of play. *Visible Language, 40*(1), 66.
Rüth, M., & Kaspar, K. (2021). Commercial video games in school teaching: Two mixed methods case studies on students' reflection processes. *Frontiers in Psychology, 11*, Article 594013.
Smuts, A. (2005). Are video games art? *Contemporary Aesthetics (Journal Archive), 3*(1), 6.
Soler-Adillon, J. (2015). El Material Intangible De l'art Interactiu: Agència, Comportament I emergència. *Artnodes*, 16.
Stalker, P. J. (2005). *Gaming in Art: a case study of two examèles of the artistic appropriation of computer games and the mapping of historical trajectories of 'art games' versus mainstream computer games*. University of the Witwatersrand, Johannesburg. Retrieved 02/09/2024 from: https://wiredspace.wits.ac.za/server/api/core/bitstreams/a1219188-e09c-4d40-a609-be58919e1941/content.
Stiles, W. B. (1993). Quality control in qualitative research. *Clinical Psychology Review, 13*(6), 593–618.
Strauss, A., & Corbin, J. (1990). *Basics of qualitative research: Techniques and procedures for developing grounded theory*. Sage.
Tavinor, G. (2023). Art and aesthetics. *The Routledge companion to video game studies*, 123–130.
Tran, M. Q., & Biddle, R. (2008). Collaboration in serious game development: a case study. In *Proceedings of the 2008 Conference on Future Play: Research, Play, Share* (pp. 49–56).
Toh, W., & Kirschner, D. (2020). Self-directed learning in video games, affordances and pedagogical implications for teaching and learning. *Computers & Education, 154*, Article 103912.
Vorderer, P., & Bryant, J. (Eds.). (2012). *Playing video games: Motives, responses, and consequences*. Routledge.

Wolf, M. J. P. (Ed.). (2001). *The medium of the video game*. University of Texas Press. https://doi.org/10.7560/791480

Wolf, M. J. P. (2010). Are video games art? In *Pop Culture Universe: Icons, Idols, Ideas*. http://popculture2.abc-clio.com/.

Wong, J. F. (2010). The text of free-form architecture: Qualitative study of the discourse of four architects. *Design Studies, 31*(3), 237–267.

Web References

https://www.sfmoma.org/exhibition/010101/ retrieved 10/09/2024.

https://whitney.org/exhibitions/bitstreams retrieved 12/09/2024.

https://www.grandpalais.fr/en/event/game-story-history-video-games-grand-palais-southeast-gallery retrieved 10/09/2024.

https://americanart.si.edu/exhibitions/games retrieved 10/09/2024.

https://www.vam.ac.uk/exhibitions/videogames retrieved 12/09/2024.

https://www1.wellesley.edu/davismuseum/whats-on/past/node/79126 retrieved 12/09/2024.

https://www.wipo.int/copyright/en/activities/video_games.html retrieved 12/09/2024.

Chapter 5
Ethics by (Game) Design

Abstract This chapter examines ethical responsibility in digital game design by foregrounding game designers' perspectives, moving beyond audience-impact approaches that dominate much of the literature. After situating ethics within the expanding cultural role of digital games and contemporary controversies, ranging from violence and representation to monetisation practices and "dark patterns", the chapter addresses the need to understand how creators interpret and manage ethical concerns within production contexts shaped by market and organisational pressures. Based on Grounded Theory analysis of designers' narrations, the chapter develops a conceptual model centred on the core category "Discussing Ethics in Video Games." Findings indicate that designers frame ethics on two interrelated levels: Ethical Issues, referring to where ethical problems are located in games, and Ethical Responsibilities, concerning who is accountable for addressing them. Ethical issues are identified both in content (e.g., stereotypes, themes aimed at reflection and awareness) and in form (e.g., choice architectures, microtransactions, and social interaction dynamics). Ethical responsibility is described as shared and negotiated: designers acknowledge a duty to reflect on potential impacts, yet resist overly prescriptive constraints that may limit creative freedom, while also attributing agency and critical responsibility to players.

5.1 Introduction: The Power of Digital Games and Their Effects on Players

This chapter explores the intersection of game design and ethical responsibility, focusing particularly on the perspectives and practices of contemporary game designers. Moving beyond player-centric approaches and audience impact studies, it turns the analytical lens toward creators themselves to understand how ethical considerations are integrated (or sidelined) within the industry production logic and creative workflows. Over the past two decades, digital games have evolved into one of the most dynamic and culturally significant forms of contemporary media. No longer confined to entertainment alone, games now inhabit an expanded space that includes education,

M. Mengoni et al., *Digital Game Design*, https://doi.org/10.1007/978-3-032-23320-2_5

health care, and professional training (Cormio et al., 2024; Laamarti et al., 2014). As the boundaries of game development continue to stretch, so too do the ethical dimensions of design and production. The digital games industry, once perceived as a niche domain driven primarily by technical innovation and entertainment goals, is now the site of active cultural negotiation, where issues of representation, economic fairness, and social impact are constantly at play (Ivory, 2015).

Within this shifting landscape, the figure of the game design has emerged as a key cultural agent. Designers today are not only technologists or artists, but also decision-makers whose choices carry ethical weight. Whether embedding subtle narratives of inclusion, designing reward systems that affect user behaviour, or negotiating market pressures and societal expectations, game designers are increasingly being called upon to consider the moral implications of their creative choices. As digital games continue to mirror and influence human realities, the question of how ethical awareness is embedded within design processes has become both urgent and unavoidable.

The digital games industry has seen remarkable growth over years, with a market revenue increasing from approximately USD 81.5 billion in 2015 to usd 197 billion in 2022, driven in part by the rise of casual games and a more diverse user base that includes educators, healthcare professionals, and people with disabilities (Ivory, 2015). Indeed, 'Digital games', including both videogames and serious games, have evolved beyond mere entertainment to serve practical purposes in fields such as education, healthcare, and training (Cormio et al., 2024). While videogames are primarily designed for entertainment and play (Newman, 2012), serious games aim to achieve specific outcomes (Laamarti et al., 2014), such cognitive training (e.g., *Le Village Aux Oiseaux*, designed for Alzheimer's patients) or education (*The Prepared Partner*, designed for childbirth education). The considerable growth of this industry worldwide has raised a renewed sensitivity towards their impact on society, especially in terms of ethical and cultural issues.

Currently, high attention is being paid to game designers' ethical responsibilities: hence, they are asked to face complex and multifaceted ethical issues over traditional technical and ludic aspects in designing. For instance, the interactivity of violence, a famous and controversial element in game studies since the early days of the discipline, has always been at the centre of a vivid debate: do violent games make people violent? How much does youth violence depend on the media they use and the increasing time they spend in front of a violent video game? Is there perhaps some responsibility on the part of game designers and production industries? Is it right to limit the interactivity of violence at the cost of reduced engagement and fun?

Effects on gamers were studied by literature as early as the 1980s, but it was not until the Columbine High School shooting in 1999 that possibilities for gamers to be affected by the normalisation of violence in entertainment culture, video games included, were introduced (Anderson et al., 2007). A meta-analysis on the relationship between violent video games and real-life physical aggression, conducted by researchers at Dartmouth College, reveals, in fact, a small increase in violent behaviours when playing violent videogames (Prescott et al., 2018). At the same time, other studies highlighted how videogames can foster people's empathy, particularly towards minorities. Shliakhovchuk's (2024) survey-based research explored the effectiveness of videogames in increasing awareness and erasing negative bias with regards to the refugee crisis. The results show an increase in empathy towards refugees. These correlations in contemporary times, however, bring us to new dynamics that have affected several entertainment industries. A term such as *woke-washing* (i.e., the exploitation of topical issues and social activism without a real intention of inclusivity) also touches videogames: the list created by the Woke Content Detector Steam Group[1], for example, consists of videoludic titles grouped by how "woke" they are. In this regard, another recent case involves *Concord*, a videogame that had a catastrophic launch after eight years of development and production. Sony, in an attempt to make up for its commercial failure, decided to remove all LGBTQAI + references in the title (Moffa, 2024). The anti-Woke list and immoral behaviours identified by distribution companies are just two elements to map inclusive game design in terms of correlations between game development and contemporary moral issues.

In addition to issues concerning the possibly negative influence of violence and the superficial inclusion of underrepresented social groups, ethical considerations even reach the impact of economic models on gamers. For example, with reference to videogame microtransactions, a very recent case study carried out by the Federal Trade Commission in USA showed the subliminal effects of video games. In particular it illustrates the case of Epic Games, the producer of *Fortnite*, that was accused of using "dark patterns", i.e., deceptive interfaces that prompt users, especially children, to make unintended or purposeful purchases without parental involvement (Federal Trade Commission, 2023).

It is therefore not surprising to realise that videogames and in general digital games are imbued with ethical and moral issues that push reflections on mistakes made and give evidence of successful strategies. Indeed, like every other form of entertainment, videogames reflect representative elements of society, in the opportunity to both photograph and influence reality. In this sense, being a mirror of today's humanity, the relationship between game designers and ethics is becoming a matter of increasing public relevance, as the videogame world is inevitably influencing cultural values, social norms and collective attitudes. For instance, serious games and gamification processes aim to respectively make education and information more interactive, and convey certain everyday experiences playfully, especially at school and in the office. These two crucial phenomena illustrate how videogaming can be an excellent lens for analysing our condition as a society and a way to predict its evolution in the coming times.

Most scientific literature limits its investigations to theoretical or case-study based reflections, mainly focusing on videogames effects on audiences, without collecting and analysing bottom-up insights from game design practitioners and producers. An exception is represented by the sociologist Wendy Grisworld (1986) who introduced the concept of the Cultural Diamond to understand the role and responsibility of game designers and the relationship between videogames and ethical design (see Fig. 5.1.)

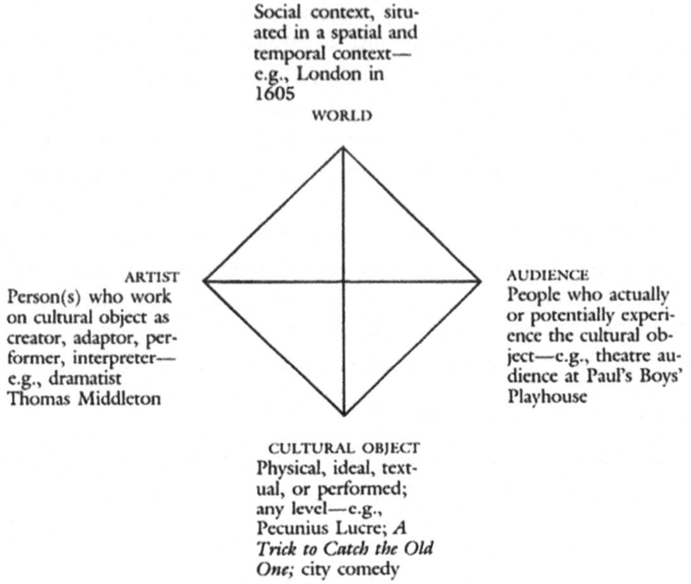

Fig. 5.1 The cultural diamond. Image from Griswold's book, "Renaissance revivals: City comedy and revenge tragedy in the London Theater, 1576–1980", p. 8

Her analysis regards any Cultural Object, whether it be a feature film, an ad, or a videogame. Each side of this diamond is mandatory for understanding said cultural object's influence on humans: the Artist, in our case, is the game designer, the World is society, and the Audience is the player (Griswold, 2012). As we mentioned earlier, there's a tendency in game studies to focus on players' behaviours or on videogames influence on society: studies taking into consideration the creators of these cultural objects (i.e. the Artist), to the best of our knowledge, are lacking.

In this frame, this chapter aims at exploring contemporary game designers' approach to the ethical challenges that are inherent to their work, by delving deeper into the complex dynamics that intertwine development processes, market requests and audience responses.

5.2 Weighting Dilemmas and Responsibilities

This section describes the results of the qualitative analysis conducted on the interviewees' narrations, in light of the emerging ethical aspects.

Game designers appear to acknowledge the dimension of ethics on two different levels. In the first place, when asked about ethics in game design, interviewees showed the tendency to identify specific aspects of video games that concretely embody and channel ethical issues (e.g., the depiction of violence, inclusive character design).

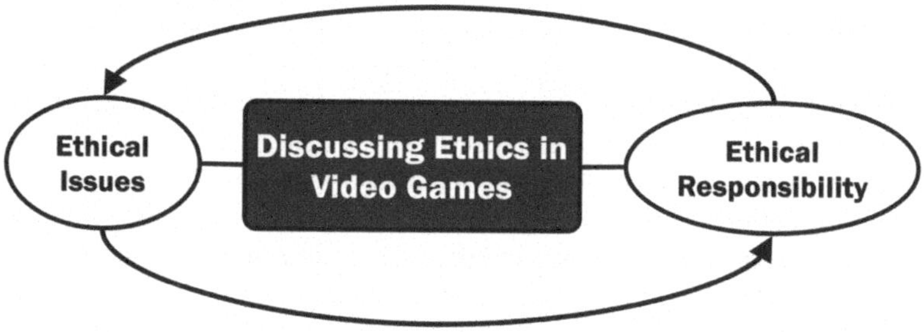

Fig. 5.2 Conceptual model of designers' perspectives on ethics and videogames. The model consists of two main categories, "Ethical Issues" and "Ethical Responsibility", which together form the core category "Discussing Ethics in Video Games"

Secondly, they shared their opinions and beliefs concerning the dynamics of ethical responsibilities, reflecting upon their professional choices as game designers and the impact of such choices on the audience once the game is delivered (i.e., considerations on video games' impact on people). Consequently, the Grounded Theory analysis of game designers' perspectives allowed the identification of the Core Category "Discussing Ethics in Video Games". The conceptual model is composed of two interrelated categories: *Ethical Issues* and *Ethical Responsibilities.* When combined together, the two categories offer a comprehensive view on interviewees' approach to ethics in game design. As the first category provides insights on the specific elements that game designers considered to be ethically problematic (i.e., where ethics lies in video games), the second category identifies ethical responsibilities and roles. As Fig. 5.2 shows, the two categories are reciprocally influencing each other (as they are connected by arrows), in that they complementarily outline game designers' thoughts on ethics in video games, establishing two separate but co-essential levels of their discourse. The *Responsibilities* category can be applied to all the items belonging to the *Issues* category, and vice versa.

The positioning of ethics in game designers' perceptions and attitudes towards their professional practice is illustrated in more detail through the identified categories and codes, described in the following subparagraphs.

5.2.1 Core Category: Discussing Ethics in Video Games

In the analysis of the opinions shared by game designers, two distinct levels of reflection were acknowledged and considered to be inherently interconnected. Indeed, when asked about the role of ethics in game design, interviewees often felt compelled to provide concrete examples and define issues of ethical relevance based on their past professional experiences. This initial reflection involved identifying directly experienced instances and practical concerns related to ethics within their workfield. However, once an ethical issue was identified, designers exhibited the tendency to define the individual or collective agent that would be held responsible for addressing such ethical concerns. In this sense, game designers are not only reflecting upon ethics in terms of theoretical values and perspectives, but are also actively engaged in considering roles and responsibilities. Specifically, they tend to dynamically consider ethical aspects in terms of intentions and potential effects, proving to perceive ethics not as a merely theoretical aspect, but rather as a concrete dimension that has the potential to impact design practices and influence design choices in the development of products. The adoption of these two complementary perspectives is encompassed in the Core Category.

5.2.2 Ethical Issues

The first category illustrates interviewees' considerations on which aspects of video games could be considered of ethical relevance according to their perspectives. Two distinct dimensions were identified in the analysis of their responses (see Table 5.1). The first dimension refers to ethical issues that appear to be connected to the content of video games (i.e., the *what* of video games), and was labelled as a sub-category named "Issues in the content". With regards to the content of video games, a small part of game designers considered ethical issues as a matter of including elements that could stimulate reflection and awareness raising (*Inputs for reflection and awareness-raising*, n = 3), such as particular storylines or the representation of specific situations that could communicate certain values (e.g., perpetuation of negative stereotypes). An even smaller portion of the interviewees stated that, in this line, not all games necessarily contain such elements. Interviewees underlined how videogames can be detached from ethical issues related to their content (*Not all games contain ethical issues*, n = 2). With reference to the second dimension, conceptualised in the sub-category "Issues in the form", game designers underlined how ethics in video games can be also detected in the modalities through which video games are experienced (i.e., the *how* of video games). The code belonging to this category, *Choices and fruition modalities* (n = 6), unfolds what game designers mean: the inclusion of microtransactions to purchase in-game benefits, the presence of numerous or scarce player customisation options, the social dynamics between players in online games are all examples of how ethics can be embedded in the fruition modalities of video games. In this context, rather than emerging in the topics a videogame deals with, ethical issues were observed in the dynamics through which it is experienced.

5.2.3 Ethical Responsibilities

The second aspect that emerged from the interviews is connected to a reflection upon the subjects which would be theoretically held responsible for the ethical impact that video games can present (see Table 5.2). In this area of reflection, interviewees

Table 5.1 Ethical Issues

Sub-category	Code	Sentences	Number of participants
Issues in the content	Inputs for reflection and awareness-raising	"[Lots of projects] are focused on ethical and awareness raising aspects, dealing with sensitive topics and social issues. When it comes to these themes, two things are important: sensitivity and clarity." (P11)	3 (27%)
	Not all games contain ethical issues	"It does not count for all games. There are video games that just wish to be simple video games." (P8)	2 (18%)
Issues in the form	Choices and fruition modalities	"The way game formats are studied can be considered ethically. For instance, a game with levels that start and end on a Playstation is different from a mobile game that keeps the kid glued to the screen. […] Some formats trigger aggressive behaviour compared to others." (P4)	6 (55%)

felt compelled to balance their own responsibilities as developers and providers with the individual responsibility of each user that interfaces with their products. The first code identified, *Designers' responsibility should be acknowledged* (n = 8), expresses the central idea that, according to interviewees, no game designer should feel completely free from any ethical reflection or restraint in their everyday work. Such an aspect suggests that, in general, ethics in game design cannot be considered as an optional aspect, but is rather embedded in the creative process. As a consequence, game designers should consider how their work has an impact on players, consciously and continuously reflecting upon ethics in their decision-making and design processes. However, game designers also expressed their concerns in prioritising ethics in their work. The code *Designers' responsibility should not be overarching* (n = 5) expresses the belief that ethical considerations should not create strict boundaries that could limit their freedom as professionals. Specifically, game designers perceived ethics as an element that could potentially limit their creative freedom. These two codes, combined together, highlight how interviewees acknowledge the importance of ethical awareness but are still not willing to follow ethical guidelines to the point that they feel strictly enforced and restricted in the imaginative and experimental aspects of game design. The tension of navigating between ethical integrity and creative freedom is pushed forward by the third code identified: *Users have responsibility* (n = 5). Indeed, game designers also underline how players have their own responsibility and role in critically reflecting upon the topics and messages expressed by videogames. In this sense, interviewees stressed the importance of engaging with video games in a thoughtful and critical manner, also acknowledging how video games do not have an educational mandate in any sense. Players, rather than passively receiving video games contents, should act as active

Table 5.2 Ethical responsibilities

Sub-category	Code	Sentences	Number of participants
Designers' responsibility	Designers' responsibility should be acknowledged	"You can sell power, for instance. […] which is also what could lead to people being addicted to your game and start spending money that they don't have […], which can quickly spiral into a huge negative impact in real life. […]. I'm happy that in the last 5–6 years the majority of game developers are thinking very carefully about how they design and develop their games so that they can be as inclusive as possible and as safe as possible." (P6)	8 (73%)
	Designers' responsibility should not be overarching	"I do consider ethical issues and I try to solve them […] without completely turning the design upside down, without altering it too much." (P10)	5 (45%)
Users'responsibility	Users have responsibility too	"You [the user] should build your critical thinking with which you can analyse a medium like a videogame or a movie. […] Ethical provocation should not be limiting a work's creative component. People should be careful about how they use video games." (P1)	5 (45%)

participants in the gaming experience, questioning underlying messages, exploring moral and ethical aspects of game's narratives and positioning themselves critically.

5.3 Implications: Ethical Game Design

As we mentioned in the introduction, nowadays' gaming landscape and Grisworld's Cultural Diamond support the importance of understanding game designers' profiles, opinions, and attitudes. Particularly now, as there is a plethora of researchers, professors, and educators who are inclined to study and use videogames to teach about real-life issues (Pallavicini et al., 2020). Karen Schrier, for example, created the EPIC framework (Schrier, 2015): it relates to seven ethics education goals (e.g. enhancing character or reflections, building ethical awareness) linked to twelve teaching strategies associated with ethics education (e.g. role-playing, simulation). Ethical considerations on game design are not only important, but mandatory when it comes to the analysis of contemporary videogames in new social contexts, whether recreational, educational, or both.

This research focused on the perspectives of game designers, uncovering how they perceive and navigate ethical issues within their profession. After analysing the theoretical framework and its results, we can affirm that within the realm of ethical issues, designers identified opportunities and concerns related to the content of videogames, such as the potential of certain storylines to raise awareness and the risk of perpetuating stereotypes. For this particular element of discussion, we mentioned earlier the rise of genres such as the serious game, which is fundamental to fully demonstrate the potential of treating ethical issues through game design. Back in 2010, a market study showed that the worldwide serious games market was worth 1.5 billion euros (Alvarez et al., 2010), as in the same period numerous studies confirmed that serious games could enhance people's awareness of social and political issues (Dallaqua et al., 2024). Defining this genre is far from simple, since many academics are split between the elements that this genre must include to be defined as such. For many, these are not designed on the basis of entertainment or enjoyment features (Michael & Chen, 2005) Also, as we can notice from the data collected, most of the interviewees do agree that game designers are responsible for the ethical dimension of their products. However, it was also acknowledged that not all games necessarily contain such ethical dimensions: casual games, which are games with a low barrier to entry and quick play sessions (International Game Developers Association, 2008), can be enjoyable even if they are not designed to teach anything. They are very successful too: "Total revenue is expected to show an annual growth rate (CAGR 2022–2029) of 8.56%, resulting in a projected market volume of US $25.86bn by 2029" (Statista, n.d.). In other words, as long as there's an ethical dimension in the product (in the storytelling, characters, dialogues), the game designers agree that it's their responsibility to approach social, political issues with the right sensitivity and attention to details.

Our study also highlighted that ethical concerns are not confined to the games' content alone, but extend to the ways in which games are experienced by players. This includes elements such as microtransactions (we mentioned the *Fortnite* controversy back in the introduction), customization options, and the social dynamics of gaming environments.

Furthermore, if the designers expressed a general consensus that they bear some level of responsibility for the ethical impact of their games (they recognized the importance of engaging in moral and ethical reflections during the design process), nearly half of our subjects also expressed concern that these ethical considerations should not overly restrict their creative freedom. This tension between maintaining ethical integrity and preserving creative autonomy emerges because, even if it's still a debated topic in game studies, videogames are considerable a contemporary art form (Smuts, 2005), so creative freedom should be assured. While designers acknowledge the necessity of considering ethics in their work, they don't always want for ethical guidelines to become so restrictive that they hinder innovation and experimentation in game design.

In addition to that, the study shed light on the belief among more than half of our subjects that players hold responsibility in critically engaging with the ethical dimensions of games. Designers suggested that while they should consider the ethical implications of their designs, players should likewise be encouraged to reflect on and question the messages conveyed by the games they interact with. As *BioShock* and *Bioshock 2*'s creative director Jordan Thomas once said in an interview about designing morality in videogames, "(…) there is no actual way to know the player's mind utterly, and so to instead use his or her behavior as a set of guidances was more attractive and more honest" (Zonn, 2010). This perspective considers the relation between players and designers and underscores the importance of active engagement and critical thinking from the players themselves. They are not passive recipients of content anymore, but rather active participants in the gaming experience: branching narrative design, for example, plays a crucial role in enhancing player engagement and immersion in video games. By allowing players to make meaningful choices that impact the story, designers can create a sense of investment and emotional connection with the game world. Interviewees highlighted how this ludic immersion is fundamental for impacting players, and using it to morally educate said players is specific to nowadays' videogame industry.

Additionally, elements of game engagement do not limit to narrative design. Microtransactions and subliminal messages have been controversial topics for decades: one of the most contemporary scandals regards, indeed, the *Fortnite* case study. The interface lets players buy in-game items like skins, emotes, and battle passes. These transactions are often framed as optional, but the game design encourages frequent purchases through limited-time offers, exclusive items, and peer pressure (*dark patterns*). Epic Games was then sued by the Federal Trade Commission and had to pay a total of $520 million to settle allegations that it collected personal data from children without first obtaining the consent of their parent or guardian (Wile, 2022). It was also accused of exposing players to bullying, threats, and harassment. Finally, ìplayers of all ages were tricked into buying online credits via what the FTC called "counterintuitive, inconsistent, and confusing" button configuration that allegedly earned Epic hundreds of millions of dollars in unauthorised charges to consumers (Wile, 2022). This case study highlights that ethical consequences of irresponsible game design (e.g., cyberbullying, unwanted in-game purchases) can lead to significant problems for young players, often without a full understanding of the real-world's financial and psychological implications. The Fortnite controversy also related to the allure of in-game rewards and the desire to enhance social status within the game community, which are permitted through a lack of attention from game designers: concerns are raised about the ethical implications of targeting players with marketing strategies designed to maximise profits through these microtransactions.

The aim of this chapter was to explore how contemporary game designers approach the ethical challenges inherent in their work, with a particular focus on their perceptions and attitudes towards ethics in the design process. The analysis revealed two interrelated categories: Ethical Issues and Ethical Responsibilities. These categories represent a two-fold tendency of game designers: they not only recognise specific ethical concerns in video games, but also reflect on their own roles in mitigating potential negative impact on players. Indeed, the theoretical framework (i.e., "Discussing Ethics in Game Design") embracing these two categories, Discussing Ethics in Video Games, underscores how ethics is not merely an abstract concern for game designers but a concrete element influencing their creative and decision-making processes. By integrating ethical considerations into their professional practices, designers demonstrate their awareness of potential cultural and social implications of videogames.

The findings suggest that ethical considerations are an integral part of the contemporary game design process, yet they are interpreted and managed in varied ways by different designers. As a result, this analysis presents a nuanced understanding of ethics in game design, illustrating that while designers are indeed aware of and concerned with ethical issues, they also face the challenge of balancing these considerations with the need for creative freedom, financial earnings, and focus on gameplay and other technical aspects of a videoludic title. By exploring the interviewees' practical point of view, the present analysis could offer a novel perspective on these topics, shedding light on the key role that game designers play (Griswold, 1986), rather than merely 'inspecting' the finished product and its potential impact.

Notes

1. https://store.steampowered.com/curator/44927664-Woke-Content-Detector/

References

Alvarez, J., Alvarez, V., Djaouti, D., & Michaud, L. (2010). *Serious games: Training & teaching-healthcare-defence & security-information & communication*. IDATE.

Anderson, C. A., Gentile, D. A. & Buckley, K. E. (2007). Violent video games: Background and overview. In *Violent Video Game Effects on Children and Adolescents: Theory, Research, and Public Policy* (pp. 3–11). Oxford University Press

Cormio, L., Agostinelli, T., & Mengoni, M. (2024). A unified framework to catalogue and classify digital games based on interaction design and validation through clustering techniques. *Multimedia Tools and Applications*, 1–21.

Dallaqua, M. F., Nunes, B., & Carvalho, M. M. (2024). Serious games research streams for social change: Critical review and framing. *British Journal of Educational Technology, 55*, 460–483.

Federal Trade Commission. (2023). *FTC Finalizes Order Requiring Fortnite maker Epic Games to Pay $245 Million for Tricking Users into Making Unwanted Charges*. https://www.ftc.gov/news-events/news/press-releases/2023/03/ftc-finalizes-order-requiring-fortnite-maker-epic-games-pay-245-million-tricking-users-making.

Griswold, W. (1986). *Renaissance revivals: City comedy and revenge tragedy in the London Theater, 1576–1980*. University of Chicago Press.

Griswold, W. (2012). *Cultures and societies in a changing world*. Sage.

International Game Developers Association (2008). *Casual game white paper*. Retrieved from https://www.org.id.tue.nl/IFIPTC14/documents/IGDACasualGames-WhitePaper-2008.pdf.

Ivory, J. D. (2015). A brief history of video games. In *The video game debate* (pp. 1–21). Routledge.

Laamarti, F., Eid, M., & El Saddik, A. (2014). An overview of serious games. *International Journal of Computer Games Technology, 2014*(1), Article 358152.

Michael, D. R., & Chen, S. L. (2005). *Serious games: Games that educate, train, and inform.* Muska & Lipman/Premier-Trade.

Moffa, A. (2024). *Concord: numeri disastrosi al lancio, Sony rimuove anche i riferimenti LGBTQ+ per aumentare le vendite.* DRCOMMODORE.it. https://www.drcommodore.it/2024/08/24/concord-lancio-negativo/

Newman, J. (2012). *Videogames.* Routledge.

Pallavicini, F., Pepe, A., Caragnano, C. C., & Mantovani, F. (2020). Video games to foster empathy: A critical analysis of the potential of Detroit: Become Human and The Walking Dead. In *International conference on human-computer interaction* (pp. 212–228). Springer International Publishing.

Prescott, A. T., Sargent, J. D., & Hull, J. G. (2018). Metaanalysis of the relationship between violent video game play and physical aggression over time. *Proceedings of the National Academy of Sciences, 115*(40), 9882–9888.

Schrier, K. (2015). EPIC: A framework for using video games in ethics education. *Journal of Moral Education, 44*(4), 393–424.

Shliakhovchuk, E. (2024). Video games as awareness raisers, attitude changers, and agents of social change. *International Journal of Computer Games Technology, 2024*(1), 3274715.

Smuts, A. (2005). Are video games art? *Contemporary Aesthetics (Journal Archive), 3*(1), 6.

Statista (n.d.). *Casual games—worldwide.* Retrieved July 30, 2025, from https://www.statista.com/outlook/amo/app/games/casual-games/worldwide

Wile R. (2022). *Fortnite maker Epic Games fined $520M after accusations it exposed young players to potential harm.* NBC News. https://www.nbcnews.com/business/consumer/fortnite-maker-epic-games-fined-520-million-accusations-exposed-child-rcna62369.

Zoss, J. M. (2010). *Ethics 101: Designing morality in games.* Game Developer. https://www.gamedeveloper.com/design/ethics-101-designing-morality-in-games.

Chapter 6
Accessibility and Inclusion in Game Design

Abstract This chapter examines digital game accessibility within the broader framework of inclusive leisure and Quality of Life, positioning videogames as culturally significant leisure opportunities with implications for social participation and rights. Drawing on perspectives from leisure studies and Special Pedagogy, the chapter frames accessibility not merely as a technical feature but as a matter of equality and inclusion within contemporary digital leisure systems. Through a Grounded Theory analysis of semi-structured interviews with game designers, the study identifies the core category *Challenges in situating inclusion between knowledge and practice*, highlighting the dynamic tension between facilitators and barriers to accessibility. Facilitators include positive recognition of accessibility as a shared responsibility and the presence of industry standards that legitimise inclusive practices. Barriers, however, emerge in the form of perceived conflicts with creative expression and structural constraints such as limited time, budget, and expertise. The findings reveal a persistent gap between value-based commitments to inclusion and their operational integration into design processes. Ultimately, the chapter argues that fostering inclusive agency and professional training is essential for transforming accessibility into a generative and systemic dimension of digital game design, capable of enhancing equitable participation and wellbeing.

6.1 Inclusive Leisure for Quality of Life: The Case of Digital Games

In recent decades, digital games have progressively established themselves as one of the most spread and socially significant forms of contemporary leisure. No longer confined to niche audiences or purely entertainment-oriented purposes, videogames are now embedded in everyday life practices and are increasingly recognised as cultural artefacts capable of shaping experiences, relationships, and meanings associated with free time (Carnicelli et al., 2016; Silk et al., 2019; Tribe, 2020). As such, digital gaming can be understood as part of a broader transformation of leisure, in which recreational activities mediated by digital technologies occupy a central

M. Mengoni et al., *Digital Game Design*, https://doi.org/10.1007/978-3-032-23320-2_6

role within contemporary societies (Hunnicutt, 2020; Schultz & McKeown, 2018; Tokarski & Zarotis, 2020). Within this evolving landscape, videogames are recognised as resources that can offer meaningful leisure experiences, supporting enjoyment, social interaction, and personal fulfilment, in line with leisure's potential to enhance individual and collective wellbeing (Kuykendall et al., 2018; Giaconi & Del Bianco, 2025).

This growing relevance of digital games as leisure practices is closely intertwined with the expansion of the leisure-related infrastructure of goods and services, which, over the past thirty years, has undergone substantial growth and diversification (Hunnicutt, 2020). Alongside this process, increased attention has been devoted to the social and cultural impact of the digital game industry, whose products and practices increasingly intersect with issues of identity, participation, and inclusion (Cormio et al., 2024; Fiore, 2022). In this sense, the consolidation of videogames within the area of leisure experiences invites a reflection that extends beyond market dynamics, calling for an analysis of their role in promoting (or, conversely, limiting) access to meaningful experiences for personal wellbeing.

At a broader level, such reflections resonate with the broader recognition of leisure as a fundamental dimension of Quality of Life and as a basic human right (UN, 2006; Giaconi, 2015; WLO, 2020; Giaconi & Del Bianco, 2025). Indeed, Article 30 of the UN Convention on the Rights of Persons with Disabilities (2006) explicitly affirms the right of people with disabilities to participate on an equal basis in cultural life, recreation, leisure, and sport, thereby highlighting the responsibility to remove barriers and to adopt appropriate measures fostering social inclusion. From this perspective, leisure can be approached through a pedagogical lens, recognising free time practices as spaces for learning, personal development, autonomy, and self-realisation (Canevaro, 2006; Giaconi, 2015; Giaconi et al., 2024a; Giaconi & Del Bianco, 2025).

Despite the widespread acknowledgement of leisure as a key indicator of societal quality of life (Tokarski & Zarotis, 2020), access to leisure opportunities remains uneven. In this direction, a substantial body of research continues to document the persistence of physical, cultural, and organisational barriers that restrict full participation for many people, including those with disabilities (Byrne, 2024; Lansdown, 2022; Roberts, 2006). With specific reference to digital leisure, scientific literature outlines an ambivalent scenario. On the one hand, digital technologies and platforms are often described as important drivers for leisure participation, as they allow for high levels of personalisation and may reduce or bypass specific environmental constraints (Boucher et al., 2010; Marques et al., 2021; Schultz & McKeown, 2018; Steinhardt et al., 2021; Yalon-Chamovitz & Weiss, 2008). Within this framework, digital gaming offers benefits that are consistent with those attributed to leisure more broadly, including opportunities for socialisation, the construction of a sense of belonging, and experiences of enjoyment and personal gratification (Cho et al., 2018; Iso-Ahola & Baumeister, 2023; Marques et al., 2021; Roy & Orazem, 2021; Sintas et al., 2015). On the other hand, however, the world of digital games still presents significant accessibility shortcomings (Anderson, 2025). Numerous studies underline how videogames frequently fail to meet universal accessibility standards, thus excluding part of the potential audience (Aguado-Delgado et al., 2020; Lee et al., 2025). These criticalities appear even more pronounced in relation to games that incorporate innovative technologies, such as eXtended Reality hardware and software, which are often introduced without an accessibility-driven perspective (Creed et al., 2024a, 2024b). In this complex scenario, accessibility in digital gaming is framed not merely as a technical issue, but rather as a matter of equality and rights protection within contemporary leisure systems (UN, 2006; Powers et al., 2015; Giaconi & Del Bianco, 2025).

In alignment with the principles of Special Pedagogy, these considerations point to the need to rethink digital leisure environments—and digital games in particular—through an explicitly inclusive perspective, encouraging policy makers, researchers, and leisure professionals to engage in the development of accessibility-oriented strategies and practices (UN, 2006; WLO, 2020; Giaconi & Del Bianco, 2025). Although existing research has addressed accessibility-related challenges in digital games (Agrimi et al., 2024; Yuan et al., 2011), there remains a substantial gap concerning the analysis of game designers' perceptions, professional cultures, and concrete design practices in relation to inclusive principles and practices. As a result, their agency in fostering inclusive digital leisure remains largely underexplored. From this standpoint, the collection of bottom-up insights into how accessibility and inclusion are conceptualised and enacted within everyday game design processes may provide a deeper understanding of both the opportunities and the constraints shaping this field, ultimately contributing to the development of a more equitable and accessible digital leisure ecosystem.

To this end, this chapter aims at analysing game designers' perceptions and practices related to accessibility and inclusion. Specifically, this chapter aims at answering the following research questions:

- RQ1: *How do game designers conceptualise accessibility and inclusion of people with disabilities in relation to their work?*
- RQ2: *How do game designers operationalise accessibility and inclusion of people with disabilities in relation to their work?*

After briefly outlining the background of this analysis, Sect. 6.2 will illustrate the results obtained from the Grounded Theory analysis of game designers' interviews in relation to this topic, following the research method detailed in Chap. 2.

6.1.1 *From Inclusive Leisure to Game Accessibility*

Digital leisure can be conceptualised as the set of leisure activities and experiences that imply a certain degree of engagement with one or more technological devices such as smartphones, computers, consoles, or networked platforms (Silk et al., 2019; Sintas et al., 2015). Accordingly, rather than constituting a homogeneous category, digital leisure encompasses a broad spectrum of practices characterised by different levels of interactivity, mediation, and technological complexity (Schultz &

McKeown, 2018). As noted by several studies on the topic (Mokhtarian et al., 2006), the field of digital leisure has grown consistently across societies, proving how Information and Communication Technologies (ICTs) play a central role for the enjoyment of leisure time, especially for younger generations. Within this context, digital games have progressively shifted from a marginal and niche form of entertainment to a central medium of digital leisure, acquiring significant cultural, social, and experiential value (Polcyn, 2018). As their diffusion has intensified, scholarly attention has increasingly turned towards the barriers that may hinder equitable access and full participation in this leisure area for all people (Agrimi et al., 2024; Anderson, 2025; Mangiron, 2012; Yuan et al., 2011).

Reflections on digital game accessibility are closely connected to the elements that constitute what has been defined as the "leisure time system" (Tokarski & Zarotis, 2020), understood as the systemic framework within which leisure activities are produced, regulated, and experienced. According to this perspective, the leisure time system encompasses multiple dimensions, including the normative elements that regulate leisure provision (such as rights, policies, and standards) (Bantekas et al., 2018), the goods and services that are related to leisure (Coalter, 2000), as well as the development of scientific and professional expertise on the various areas of leisure (Coalter, 1997). From this standpoint, promoting equity in leisure participation requires the construction of an inclusive and integrated leisure time system (Schleien et al., 1996), grounded in shared knowledge, collective awareness, and coordinated actions aimed at ensuring equal opportunities to engage in free time pursuits, including digital games.

Within the field of game studies, accessibility research has predominantly concentrated on the dimension of products and services, with a particular focus on identifying the barriers that players may encounter during gameplay. These barriers are commonly associated with challenges in perceiving game stimuli, selecting appropriate in-game responses, or providing input through interaction devices, and research efforts have largely been directed towards proposing technical solutions to mitigate such challenges (Agrimi et al., 2024; Mangiron, 2012; Yuan et al., 2011). Early and influential contributions in this area have therefore adopted a predominantly technical and design-oriented approach, seeking to systematise accessibility issues and to translate them into actionable design recommendations. In particular, many studies have relied on interaction models that conceptualise gameplay as a sequence of interconnected phases—receiving information, determining responses, and executing actions through input mechanisms—each of which may be experienced differently by players (Anderson, 2025).

Within this framework, several accessibility guidelines have been developed to support inclusive game design. These include, for example, recommendations to provide multimodal feedback by combining visual, auditory, and haptic cues; to implement adaptable input systems that allow players to remap controls or use alternative devices; to reduce or customise time-based constraints that may disadvantage some users; and to offer adjustable difficulty levels and personalised interface settings. These efforts have played a key role in shaping accessibility guidelines addressed to game developers, supporting the integration of inclusive features within commercial and independent game productions (Westin et al., 2011). At the same time, however, the literature has also highlighted the limitations of guideline-based approaches, noting that accessibility recommendations are often difficult to apply uniformly across different game genres, interaction paradigms, and production contexts. In particular, it has been argued that game development differs substantially from other software design domains, as it is deeply intertwined with entertainment value, challenge, narrative engagement, and player experience, elements that may complicate the straightforward adoption of accessibility solutions (Anderson, 2025).

While this body of work has been instrumental in establishing game accessibility as a legitimate and recognised research area, as well as in providing concrete and operational design knowledge, it has largely focused on identifying which accessibility strategies exist and how they can be technically implemented (Powers et al., 2015). As a consequence, limited attention has been devoted to the perspectives of game designers themselves, especially with regard to how accessibility is understood, interpreted, negotiated, and prioritised within everyday professional practices, thereby foregrounding their role and agency as digital leisure professionals. The processes through which accessibility-related knowledge is translated into design decisions and embedded within inclusive leisure experiences therefore remain insufficiently explored. To this end, investigating designers' perspectives can offer valuable insights into how accessibility considerations are shaped by professional cultures, production contexts, and creative approaches, ultimately contributing to a more comprehensive understanding of digital game accessibility and inclusion processes.

6.2 In Between Facilitators and Barriers

This section reports the findings of the qualitative analysis carried out in relation to game designers' perceptions in relation to accessibility and inclusion. The Grounded Theory analysis of participants' narrations led to the identification of the core category *Challenges in situating inclusion between knowledge and practice*, which captures the complex and often contradictory dynamics experienced by game designers when addressing the inclusion of players with disabilities within digital game design. This core category reflects a condition of tension in which elements that potentially support accessibility coexist with factors that, conversely, hinder its full and systematic implementation in everyday professional practices. Such a tension unfolds at the intersection between what designers know, value, or recognise as important, and what they are concretely able to enact within the constraints of their work contexts, as visually synthesised in Fig. 6.1. Within the resulting conceptual framework, two opposing yet interrelated main categories were identified: *Facilitators for accessibility* and *Barriers to accessibility*. Together, these categories articulate the central dichotomy emerging from designers' narratives with regard to their perceptions, practices, and professional decision-making processes. On the one hand, the category of *Facilitators for accessibility* encompasses those elements that sustain and legitimise designers' inclusive agency, such as the recognition of accessibility as a fundamental dimension of everyday life and of digital leisure. On the other hand, the category of *Barriers to accessibility* brings to our attention the factors that constrain or limit the translation of accessibility principles into concrete design choices, including structural and organisational aspects such as limited budgets, time pressures, or production priorities. Importantly, the tension between facilitators and barriers operates on two interconnected levels, involving both the ways in which accessibility is conceptually framed and the ways in which it is operationalised within professional practice. As illustrated in Fig. 6.1, the two main categories are represented as circles arranged along a concentric trajectory, symbolised by two discontinuous arrows forming a circular movement. This visual representation is intended to convey the idea that facilitators and barriers are not mutually exclusive, but rather coexist within participants' perspectives in a dynamic and evolving balance. Along the trajectory of each main category, its two corresponding subcategories are positioned, reflecting the internal articulation of each dimension. Two-sided arrows connect the subcategories in pairs, which are placed in opposition to one another so as to mirror their counterparts. This arrangement highlights the parallel structure between facilitators and barriers, as well as their alignment across different levels of reference (the conceptual one and the operational one).

The core category *Challenges in situating inclusion between knowledge and practice* encapsulates the central processes emerging from game designers' narratives concerning the inclusion of players with disabilities within digital games. Rather than pointing to specific design outputs or to stable and codified sets of practices, this core category is intended to reflect participants' understanding of inclusion as

Fig. 6.1 Conceptual framework showing the core category "Challenges in situating inclusion between knowledge and practice", reflected by the two main categories "Facilitators for accessibility" and "Barriers to accessibility"

a situated, ongoing, and inherently dynamic process. From the designers' perspective, inclusion is described as something that unfolds through continuous negotiation within everyday professional activity in the leisure field, shaped by the interaction of multiple and often competing forces. In this sense, their accounts highlight how inclusion requires an intentional and reflective form of agency, configuring itself less as a set of predefined actions to be implemented and more as a professional stance that is constantly redefined through encounters with both available resources and persistent constraints.

At the core of this category lies a structural duality that generates a relational tension, deeply influencing how accessibility (and, more broadly, inclusion) is conceptualised and enacted in professional practice. Indeed, accessibility emerges in designers' narratives as positioned at the intersection between what is known and considered meaningful at a conceptual level, and what is materially and organisationally feasible at an operational level. As a result, designers appear to move repeatedly back and forth between intentions and opportunities, ideals and compromises, as well as between *knowing* and *doing*. This oscillation reflects the complexity of translating inclusive values into concrete design choices within real-world production contexts.

Within this framework, the duality between facilitators and barriers operates simultaneously across two interconnected levels. On a conceptual level, it shapes designers' perceptions, attitudes, and interpretative frameworks related to accessibility. It highlights how inclusion is understood, how it is perceived in relation to creativity and game experience, and why it is considered relevant or not within game design. On an operational level, the same tension informs concrete design processes and practices, influencing how accessibility principles are translated into specific features, settings, workflows, or, alternatively, how they are downplayed, postponed, or only partially implemented due to contextual constraints, as will be later illustrated.

As the dynamic processes encompassed by the core category unfold through the interaction of the two interrelated dimensions that correspond to the main categories of the conceptual framework (*Facilitators for accessibility* and *Barriers to accessibility*), the inherent duality of promoting inclusion becomes visible in designers' narratives and takes on an actionable form. Importantly, within this analytical framework, facilitators and barriers do not appear as static, clearly delimited, or mutually exclusive domains. Rather, they coexist and continuously interact within everyday professional reality, as evidenced by participants' accounts. Supporting and constraining factors are therefore rarely encountered in isolation, suggesting that accessibility is often simultaneously enabled and restricted through the interplay of individual attitudes, knowledge, and competencies, as well as broader structural and organisational conditions.

6.2.1 Facilitators for Accessibility

The first key dynamic emerging from designers' narratives concerns the set of elements that support, enable, and legitimise accessibility-oriented practices, fostering a general inclination towards inclusive processes within digital game design. These elements reflect both the symbolic validation of accessibility as a legitimate professional concern and the availability of practical resources that designers can mobilise in their everyday work. As such, *Facilitators for accessibility* encompasses those conditions that sustain designers' inclusive agency, operating at both a cultural and an operational level. This main category is articulated into two subcategories: "Positive recognition" and "Presence of standards" (Table 6.1).

The first subcategory, "Positive recognition", refers to the shared and explicit acknowledgement among designers of accessibility as a meaningful, necessary, and legitimate dimension of game design. This recognition is grounded both in ethical considerations and in an understanding of play as a cultural and social leisure experience that should be accessible to all. Participants frequently framed accessibility as a matter that intersects with designers' individual responsibility as leisure professionals and with the broader protection of rights related to social inclusion and cultural participation (Code: "Perceiving accessibility as a responsibility and means for social inclusion", n = 9). In this respect, one designer stated that "It is our responsibility to overcome as many digital barriers as possible and therefore expand access to the product to the fullest extent permitted by existing technical possibilities"

Table 6.1 Facilitators for accessibility

Sub-category	Code	Sub-code	Sentences
Positive recognition	Perceiving accessibility as a responsibility and means for social inclusion	"Games are democratic, everyone should have access to videogames just like everyone has the right to access art" (P2) "I find it emotionally moving to open a menu and find all those options for people who are sensitive to contrast, colours, and so on; it is something truly remarkable and impressive" (P10)	9 (82%)
	Considering accessibility as a dimension that concerns all	"These things matter even if you don't have a disability" (P6) "[accessibility] is not necessarily only for people with disabilities" (P7)	5 (45%)
Presence of standards	Recognising the relevance of existing standards	"Luckily, today disabilities are not a barrier in the world of videogames anymore" (P1) "Today there are standards that are more or less expected: subtitles, colour-blind settings, audio options—these things have become normal" (P7)	6 (55%)
	Complying to standards as minimum baseline	"There are guidelines and examples we can look at, especially in bigger productions, that show what can be done" (P9) "To do so we make use of different accessibility protocols, such as the use of high legibility fonts, text to speech, high contrast, etc." (P11)	8 (73%)

(P11), aligning game accessibility with fundamental principles of cultural democracy. Similarly, another participant remarked that adopting an accessibility-oriented approach is perceived as an investment in participation, diversity, and social impact, rather than as a purely technical adjustment. This aspect appeared to be felt by some participants also at an emotional level. For instance, one designer stated that they "find it emotionally moving to open a menu and find all those options for people who are sensitive to contrast, colours, and so on; it is something truly remarkable and impressive" (P10).

Moreover, accessibility was consistently described as a concern that extends beyond specific impairments or marginal situations, instead addressing a broader and more heterogeneous population of players (Code: "Considering accessibility as a dimension that concerns all", n = 5). In this sense, designers repeatedly stressed that "actually, accessibility-related features emerge in response to a specific need, but some of them [...] end up becoming a standard useful to all" (P8), as promoting inclusive processes implies design choices that can support a wide range of situations, preferences, and playing conditions. Participants also supported this view through practical examples, underlining how gameplay needs and constraints vary across individuals and "[these] choices impact on who will be able to enjoy the ludic experience we are preparing" (P9). Through these accounts, designers' narratives reinforce the conceptualisation of accessibility as a universal dimension of human experience, rather than as a mere exceptional or compensatory measure.

The second subcategory, "Presence of standards", captures designers' awareness of existing accessibility standards within the game industry and the ways in which these regulatory and normative elements concretely shape the implementation of accessibility features in their projects. Participants widely acknowledged that accessibility has gained increasing visibility and legitimacy within the videogame industry (Code: "Recognising the relevance of existing standards", n = 6), particularly through platform requirements. As one designer explained, "Platforms themselves require certain compliance rules if you want to publish" (P2), framing standards as a structural indicator that accessibility is no longer perceived as marginal, but rather as institutionally recognised.

In addition to their symbolic value, standards were also described as practical reference points that actively guide design decisions and workflows (Code: "Complying to standards as minimum baseline", n = 8). Designers commonly referred to the inclusion of features such as command remapping, adjustable subtitles, audio controls, colour contrast options, and scalable text as baseline requirements, "so that commands can be used by everyone" (P8). In this regard, participants also highlighted how the growing presence of accessibility within digital game industry discourse provides them with concrete models and resources to draw upon, noting that "We are more than happy to comply with the standards of the various platforms, to get informed in the first place to try including everyone" (P2). Overall, the presence of standards emerges as both a legitimising framework and an operational scaffold that supports the translation of inclusive intentions into tangible design practices.

6.2.2 *Barriers to Accessibility*

The second key dynamic emerging from designers' narratives concerns the set of factors that were identified as hindering or constraining the adoption of accessibility-oriented practices within digital game–related leisure. Across participants' accounts, these elements most prominently include the difficulty of reconciling accessibility solutions with creative and authorial expression, as well as structural limitations related to the availability of resources such as time, budget, and specialised expertise. Together, these aspects delineate the category Barriers to accessibility, which is articulated into two subcategories: "Creativity conflict" and "Lack of resources" (Table 6.2).

The first subcategory, "Creativity conflict", captures designers' perceptions of accessibility as a potential source of tension within the creative process. In several narratives, accessibility requirements were described as necessary and ethically relevant, yet simultaneously as constraints that might interfere with the aesthetic coherence, genre conventions, or intended "identity" of a game (Code: "Perceiving accessibility as a limit to creativity", n = 5). For instance, one participant explained that, in their opinion, "accessibility should not destroy a product, it should rather allow everyone to engage with it" (P2), expressing concerns that accessibility may be experienced as an externally imposed obligation rather than as an intrinsic design approach aimed at fostering equitable participation. Within this framing, some designers reported perceiving compliance with accessibility requirements as a risk of diluting, compromising, or reshaping their original creative vision.

Alongside this perceived creative tension, accessibility was also positioned by some participants as a secondary or optional component of the design process (Code: "Not considering accessibility as a priority", n = 4), particularly when compared with other competing priorities such as narrative coherence, visual style,

Table 6.2 Barriers to accessibility

Sub-category	Code	Sub-code	Sentences
Creativity conflict	Perceiving accessibility as a limit to creativity	"Inclusivity should not be forced, it has to bring value; otherwise it becomes a double-edged sword" (P3)	4 (36%)
	Not considering accessibility as a priority	"Besides being a cost, it does not even bring visibility, so those who do it do so because they believe it is the right thing to do" (P4) "We do what we can, but it's not something we can always put at the centre" (P8)	5 (45%)
Lack of resources	Recognising constraints related to accessibility implementation	"We simply don't have the means to do everything; we don't have the budget, the time, or the people" (P1) "There are companies that can afford teams of ten or twenty people working only on accessibility: we clearly cannot" (P3)	10 (91%)

6.3 Implications: Promoting Inclusive Trajectories

The findings obtained through this analysis appear to be providing interesting insights on the debate of accessibility and inclusion within digital game design, offering a unique perspective on game designers' inclusive agency.

In general, designers' views appear to draw on what can be defined as an ecological approach to disability (WHO, 2001), acknowledging the relational and situated nature of accessibility (Titchkosky, 2011) and highlighting the interdependence between players' needs and game environments. Within this framework, game designers' narratives can be interpreted as consistent with the interpretation of inclusion as the outcome of the dynamic interactions between the individual and the environment in which leisure experiences take place. In this direction, designers themselves recognise how inclusive processes can be understood as something emerging from the continuous interaction between people and their environments, rather than from compensatory actions targeted solely at the individual (Bronfenbrenner, 2000; WHO, 2001; Giaconi, 2015).

In the first place, the analysis of the interviews revealed how, by framing digital game accessibility as a responsibility and fundamental dimension for engagement, game designers' share a positive view on inclusive design practices within professional discourse. As this shared understanding fosters a more favourable attitude towards accessibility-oriented choices, it is possible to affirm how participants were found to be aligned with the idea that barriers to participation are not fixed or inevitable, but are produced—and potentially transformed—through design choices, organisational arrangements, and cultural assumptions embedded in life contexts, including leisure ones (Canevaro, 1986; Giaconi et al., 2024a). This picture is further in harmony with the interpretation of participation as the result of dynamic intersection between personal motivations and preferences, habits and social roles, skills and contextual factors (Haythorne et al., 2022; Heister et al., 2023; Marques et al., 2021), calling for the need to rethink and redesign digital leisure experiences such as playing videogames as constitutional dimensions of everyday life and personal wellbeing (Di Marino et al., 2018; Heister et al., 2023). Such a sensitivity overcomes the idea of leisure as a marginal or optional dimension, encompassing instances related to identity, cultural participation, and social inclusion, therefore embracing a rights-based approach that recognises access to leisure, recreation, and cultural life as fundamental human rights (Bantekas et al., 2018; WLO, 2020). From this standpoint, game designers appeared to be aware of how digital games can represent a space for social connection and sense of community belonging. Additionally, by explicitly addressing how accessibility is relevant to everyone and can produce benefits for all people, game designers proved to be adopting an approach that recognises and values diversity, interpreting it as a foundational dimension for social inclusion, rather than a technical add-on or optional enhancement (Titchkosky, 2011). In this sense, positive recognition functions as a key conceptual resource for inclusive agency, shaping how inclusion can be valued, justified, and prioritised within game design practices. At the same time, designers addressed the positive influence of the normative dimension or gameplay innovation. In this regard, designers stated that accessibility is "not something I think of obsessively" (P10), portraying accessibility as a desirable yet non-essential dimension of game development. These accounts do not simply indicate resistance to inclusion: rather, they reveal how accessibility is hierarchised within professional decision-making processes, negotiated alongside other creative and production-related concerns.

The second subcategory, "Lack of resources", captures how designers explicitly acknowledge the structural and organisational constraints that circumscribe the practical enactment of accessibility within game design work. In participants' accounts, accessibility is rarely framed as a purely design-driven choice: rather, it is repeatedly described as contingent upon the availability of concrete resources, most notably time, financial investment, and human capital (Code: Recognising constraints related to accessibility implementation, n = 10). Among these constraints, time emerges as a particularly critical factor, with designers emphasising how accessibility-related features tend to accumulate as additional tasks within already demanding production schedules. As one participant observed, "development times keep getting longer, and adding more features means adding more work that someone has to do" (P5), underscoring how accessibility is often perceived as intensifying existing workload pressures. Alongside temporal constraints, financial limitations appeared to play a central role in shaping accessibility-related decisions as well. Participants frequently point to the difficulty of allocating economic resources to accessibility when its return on investment is perceived as uncertain or indirect, a concern that is especially pronounced in small or independent studios. This tension between ethical commitment and economic sustainability is articulated clearly in designers' reflections. As one participant explained, "if I had a bigger team and more money, I would absolutely do more, but in reality that's not possible" (P10), highlighting how accessibility initiatives are often driven by individual values rather than supported by stable financial structures. In addition to time and budget, constraints related to human resources and expertise further appeared to delimit what can realistically be achieved. Designers repeatedly stressed the absence of specialised roles or dedicated competencies within their teams, contrasting their own contexts with those of larger companies. As one participant noted, "we try to do what we can, because of course we would also like to include many accessibility options, but we are aware of our limits. We do not always know who to ask or how to implement them properly" (P7). Such comparisons seem to hint at the idea that comprehensive accessibility implementation is unevenly distributed across the industry and, at the same time, closely tied to organisational scale.

Overall, these narratives illustrate how limited resources function not merely as external obstacles, but as structuring conditions that shape designers' assessments of feasibility and sustainability in their professional work. Therefore, the lack of resources represents one of the elements that most prominently contributes to defining the boundaries of accessibility practices, embedding inclusion within the material realities of everyday professional environments.

embedded in the leisure time system, by underlining how digital game design, rather than being the outcome of isolated individual decisions, is part of a broader approach endorsed by the game industry. In this sense, participants proved to be aware of the interrelated dimensions that contribute to shaping the experience of digital games, framing their professional action with a systemic view. Designers' recurrent reference to accessibility standards and platform requirements prove how accessibility is legitimised and promoted by the video game industry, signalling a cultural change oriented towards the increase of equal participation opportunities (Aitchison, 2009). These considerations can help us understand how accessibility is framed as a shared responsibility, and does not rely solely on individual profession: it is embedded in a system that brings together technological innovation, cultural values and regulatory actions. In continuity with these reflections, a relevant insight emerging from the analysis concerns the importance attributed to the application of shared accessibility measures, which shows how participants value concrete examples, shared knowledge and established solutions as a baseline for inclusive design actions.

Despite recognising accessibility as an important dimension and proving to be aware of its implications in terms of social participation, almost half of participants shared how, when it comes to concrete implementation, it can become a residual aspect. The conceptual framing of *accessibility* and *aesthetics* as opposing dimensions, which emerges from participants' narratives, suggests that game designers may perceive compliance with accessibility standards as a potential threat to personal creative expression, raising concerns about a possible "flattening" of the designed product and experience. In this view, participants lacked the interpretation of accessibility as a perspective that can foster creative exploration, associating it with the risk of standardising their works. Consequently, while all participants articulate accessibility as a central value in game design, not all appear willing to fundamentally reconsider their creative processes in light of inclusive principles. This perspective points to a persistent gap between the recognition of accessibility at the level of values and its integration at the level of design practice. More specifically, it reveals a limited adoption of accessibility-by-design approaches, whereby accessibility is embedded from the earliest stages of ideation (Kim et al., 2021; Ormerod & Newton, 2005). Instead, designers might appear to be framing accessibility as a set of subsequent adjustments or compensatory modifications, perceived as external to the core creative vision and potentially intrusive to authorial intent. Such an understanding positions accessibility as an intervention that constrains creativity, rather than as a generative design stance capable of informing and enriching creative processes from the outset (Steen, 2013; Titchkosky, 2011). This element of reflection represents an interesting outcome of the study, as it seems to expose the distance between value-based commitments to inclusion and the concrete conditions under which game design practices take place, suggesting that accessibility, on the operational level, somehow becomes a negotiable aspect. The contradiction between the recognition of accessibility as an important dimension and its uneven operationalisation becomes intelligible when considering designers' mention of significant lacks in terms of resources. In this direction, the findings suggest that deprioritisation takes place when accessibility-related needs are confronted with competing demands such a tight production schedules, limited budgets, lack of specialised expertise, and market pressures. This dynamic is consistent with scientific literature, which shows how the concrete possibilities of implementing accessible and inclusive processes are often constrained by organisational routines and economic rationales, resulting in partial or uneven forms of participation (Shields & Synnot, 2016; Steinhardt et al., 2021). As a result, findings suggest how accessibility, at times, risks to be perceived by game designers as an added burden rather than as an integral dimension of design quality, especially in professional contexts characterised by limited resources and production capacity. Leisure studies literature highlights how such perceptions contribute to the marginalisation of inclusive practices, particularly when organisational cultures do not explicitly value or reward accessibility-related efforts (Blackshaw, 2016). Interpreted within this framework and complex scenario, the apparent contradiction between values and practices does not indicate a lack of awareness, but rather reveals the structural and cultural conditions that can shape designers' decision-making. As a consequence, inclusive processes in game design appear to be deeply situated within the complexity of game designers' space of action.

Overall, the obtained results allow us to make some final considerations related to game designers' attitudes and practices in relation to accessibility and inclusion of players with disabilities.

In the first place, results highlight the importance of fostering inclusive agency (Aiello & Giaconi, 2024; Giaconi et al., 2025) as a means through which game designers, and leisure professionals in general, can act intentionally towards inclusion, bringing together personal awareness with both knowledge and practical know-how. Indeed, our analysis shows that game designers' inclusive agency is neither fixed nor guaranteed. Rather, it emerges as a dynamic achievement which is shaped by personal assumptions, possessed knowledge and environmental factors, which constitute the material and symbolic resources they have at their disposal to promote accessibility-driven design processes. These considerations ultimately highlight the importance of inclusive training as a crucial lever for the acquisition of proper theoretical and practical tools to implement accessibility in game design, leading game designers to become key facilitators themselves. In this sense, the lack of inclusive training can, in fact, translate into negligent attitudes, generating invisible barriers that can hinder inclusive processes even when time and budget related resources are available (Marques et al., 2021; Shields & Synnot, 2016). In this regard, as professional training represents a "crucial channel for inclusive implementation" (Giaconi et al., 2024b, p. 46), it can also guide organisations and companies, promoting systemic change towards inclusive approaches. Accordingly, inclusive training can serve as a transformative learning opportunity, aligning professional practices with shared visions on inclusion while ensuring that accessibility can be sustained and continuously improved across digital game design contexts.

In the second place, an element that was notably not mentioned by any participant is that of co-design, to be interpreted as a process of "joint inquiry and imagination" aimed at allowing multiple actors to "jointly bring about positive change" (Steen, 2013, pp. 27–28). In this context, co-design does not merely represent a methodological pathway to develop accessible solutions, but rather a pedagogical process aimed at actively engaging people with disabilities in reimagining how digital games can be made more accessible, empowering their perspectives and creating a shared space for dialogue and knowledge sharing (Giaconi et al., 2021, 2024a; Santilli, 2025). From a pedagogical standpoint, the integration of co-design represents both a conceptual and operational resource, allowing game designers to meet the lived experiences of people with disabilities and promoting a generative approach in which creativity is not limited but rather enriched (Titchkosky, 2011). Such a dialogic process can frame the principles of accessibility in their dynamic and relational value (Del Bianco et al., 2024; May, 2024; Sarmiento-Pelayo, 2015; Shogren et al., 2022), offering novel opportunities for game designers in relation to the promotion of context-specific inclusive practices.

In conclusion, this chapter allowed us to reflect on game designers' attitudes and practices in relation to accessibility and inclusion of players with disability, situating designers' perspectives in contemporary debates linked to leisure, active participation, and social inclusion. By evidencing the dynamics that emerge at the intersection between personal beliefs, existing standards, creative needs and external constraints, a complex and rich perspective was built out of participants' narrations and lived experiences, expressing how the removal of barriers within digital game experiences does not represent a mere technical adjustment, but hints at an intentional, pedagogical act aimed at recognising diversity and ensuring equal opportunities for participation. To this end, situating accessibility within the lived experiences of game designers offered us a more nuanced understanding of how inclusion is produced, regulated, and constrained in everyday professional scenarios, ultimately indicating the trajectories through which digital game design can be transformed into a concrete opportunity for Quality of Life and authentic involvement of people with disabilities (Giaconi, 2015; Giaconi & Del Bianco, 2025).

References

Agrimi, E., Battaglini, C., Bottari, D., Gnecco, G., & Leporini, B. (2024). Game accessibility for visually impaired people: A review. *Soft Computing, 28*(17), 10475–10489.

Aguado-Delgado, J., Gutierrez-Martinez, J. M., Hilera, J. R., De-Marcos, L., & Otón, S. (2020). Accessibility in video games: A systematic review. *Universal Access in the Information Society, 19*(1), 169–193.

Aiello, P., Giaconi, C. (2024). *L'agire inclusivo. Interfacce pedagogiche e didattiche.* Manuale per l'insegnante, Brescia, Morcelliana Scholé.

Aitchison, C. (2009). Exclusive discourses: Leisure studies and disability. *Leisure Studies, 28*(4), 375–386.

Anderson, S. L. (2025). The ground floor approach to video game accessibility: Identifying design features prioritized by accessibility reviews. *Games and Culture, 20*(6), 748–759.

Bantekas, I., Stephenson Chow, P. Y., Karapapa, S., Polymenopoulou, E. (2018). Participation in cultural life, recreation, leisure, and sport. In I. Bantekas, M. A. Stein, D. Anastasiou (Eds.), *The UN Convention on the Rights of Persons with Disabilities: A Commentary. Oxford Commentaries on International Law, Oxford, Oxford Academic*, pp. 863–923.

Blackshaw, T. (2016). *Re-imagining leisure studies.* Routledge.

Boucher, N., Dumas, F., Maltais, D. B., & Richards, C. L. (2010). The influence of selected personal and environmental factors on leisure activities in adults with cerebral palsy. *Disability and Rehabilitation, 32*(16), 1328–1338.

Bronfenbrenner, U. (2000). *Ecological systems theory.* American Psychological Association.

Byrne, S. (2024). The right to leisure for children with disabilities: Towards greater awareness and implementation. *International Journal of the Sociology of Leisure, 7*, 369–390.

Canevaro, A. (1986). *Handicap e identità.* Cappelli.

Canevaro, A. (2006). *Le logiche del confine e del sentiero. Una pedagogia dell'inclusione (per tutti, disabili inclusi).* Trento, Erickson.

Carnicelli, S., McGillivray, D., & McPherson, G. (2016). *Digital leisure cultures: Critical perspectives.* Taylor & Francis.

Cho, D., Post, J., & Kim, S. K. (2018). Comparison of passive and active leisure activities and life satisfaction with aging. *Geriatrics & Gerontology International, 18*(3), 380–386.

Coalter, F. (1997). Leisure sciences and leisure studies: Different concept, same crisis? *Leisure Sciences, 19*(4), 225–268.

Coalter, F. (2000). Public and commercial leisure provision: Active citizens and passive consumers? *Leisure Studies, 19*(3), 163–181.

Cormio, L., Giaconi, C., Mengoni, M., Santilli, T. (2024). Exploring game design approaches through conversations with designers. *Design Studies, 91–92* n. C. https://doi.org/10.1016/j.destud.2024.101253.

Creed, C., Al-Kalbani, M., Theil, A., Sarcar, S., & Williams, I. (2024a). Inclusive AR/VR: Accessibility barriers for immersive technologies. *Universal Access in the Information Society, 23*(1), 59–73.

Creed, C., Al-Kalbani, M., Theil, A., Sarcar, S., & Williams, I. (2024b). Inclusive augmented and virtual reality: A research agenda. *International Journal of Human-Computer Interaction, 40*(20), 6200–6219.

Del Bianco, N., D'Angelo, I., Caldarelli, A., Shogren, K. A., & Giaconi, C. (2024). Co-designing inclusive museums with people with intellectual disabilities: A pilot study in immersive virtual environments. *The International Journal of the Inclusive Museum, 18*(1), 63–81.

Di Marino, E., Tremblay, S., Khetani, M., & Anaby, D. (2018). The effect of child, family and environmental factors on the participation of young children with disabilities. *Disability and Health Journal, 11*(1), 36–42.

Fiore, P. (2022). *I videogiochi in Italia valgono 2,2 miliardi di euro.* AGI. Retrieved from: https://www.agi.it/economia/news/2022-03-25/videogiochi-italia-dati-valore-16122533/

Giaconi, C., Ascenzi, A., Del Bianco, N., D'angelo, I., & Capellini, S. A. (2021). Virtual and Augmented Reality: A Pilot Study. *The International Journal of the Inclusive Museum, 14*(1), 95–106.

Giaconi, C., Del Bianco, N., D'Angelo, I., Borsini, L., Ceccacci, S., Shogren, K. A. (2024a). Museum accessibility and people with disabilities: the challenge of co-designing pathways. *Giornale Italiano di Educazione alla Salute, Sport e Didattica Inclusiva, 8*, 1–21.

Giaconi C., Taddei A., Del Bianco N., D'Angelo I. (2024b). La Pedagogia Speciale oggi: ripartire dalle orme di Andrea Canevaro per ritrovarsi Comunità. In Società Italiana di Pedagogia Speciale (SIPeS) (Ed.), *L'inclusione non si ferma. Cammina sempre* (pp. 41–53). Volume in ricordo di Andrea Canevaro, Trento, Erickson.

Giaconi, C., Del Bianco, N. (2025). *La Pedagogia Speciale per il Progetto di Vita.* Lecce, Pensa Multimedia.

Giaconi, C. (2015). *Qualità della Vita e adulti con disabilità. Percorsi di ricerca e prospettive inclusive.* Milano, FrancoAngeli.

Haythorne, R., Gega, L., Knapp, P., & Crawford, H. (2022). What are the barriers and facilitators to participation in active recreation for people with learning disabilities? A scoping review. *British Journal of Learning Disabilities, 50*(3), 350–363.

Heister, N., Zentel, P., & Köb, S. (2023). Participation in everyday leisure and its influencing factors for people with intellectual disabilities: A scoping review of the empirical findings. *Disabilities, 3*(2), 69–294.

Hunnicutt, B. (2020). *The age of experiences*. Temple University Press.

Iso-Ahola, S. E., Baumeister, R. F. (2023). Leisure and meaning in life. *Frontiers in Psychology, 14*, 1074649.

Kim, N. W., Joyner, S. C., Riegelhuth, A., & Kim, Y. (2021). Accessible visualization: Design space, opportunities, and challenges. *Computer graphics forum, 40*(3), 173–188.

Kuykendall, L., Boemerman, L., & Zhu, Z. (2018). The importance of leisure for subjective well-being. In E. Diener, S. Oishi, & L. Tay (Eds.), *Handbook of well-being* (pp. 1–14). DEF Publishers.

Lansdown, G. (2022). Article 31: The rights to rest, play, recreation, and cultural and artistic activities. Children's Well-Being: Indicators and ResearchIn Z. Vaghri, J. Zermatten, G. Lansdown, & B. Ruggiero (Eds.), *Monitoring State Compliance with the UN Convention on the Rights of the Child* (Vol. 25, pp. 271–280). Cham.

Lee, M., Yeomans, M., Lansford, E., & Kuo, H. J. (2025). Benefits, barriers, and accessibility in video games: a focus group study of college students with disabilities. *Disability and Rehabilitation: Assistive Technology*, 1–16.

Mangiron, C. (2012). Exploring new paths towards game accessibility. *Approaches to Translation Studies*, 36.

Marques, J. S., Regalado, I. C., Galvão, É. R. V. P., Ferreira, H. N., Longo, E., Lindquist, A. R. R. (2021). Participation in leisure activities from the perception of children with disabilities and their families in Brazil. *Journal of Rehabilitation Medicine, 53*(1), jrm00136.

May, E. (2024). Critical pedagogy and disability in participatory research: a review. *Information and Learning Sciences*, 125(7/8), 437–455.

Mokhtarian, P. L., Salomon, I., & Handy, S. L. (2006). The impacts of ICT on leisure activities and travel: A conceptual exploration. *Transportation, 33*(3), 263–289.

Ormerod, M. G., & Newton, R. A. (2005). Briefing for accessibility in design. *Facilities, 23*(7/8), 285–294.

Polcyn, S. (2018). The evolution of free time throughout history. Video games as a modern leisure activity. *Biuletyn Historii Wychowania, 38*, 187–200.

Powers, G., Nguyen, V., & Frieden, L. (2015). Video game accessibility: A legal approach. *Disability Studies Quarterly, 35*(1).

Roberts, K. (2006). *Leisure in contemporary societies*. Wallingford, CABI International.

Roy, S., Orazem, P. F. (2021). Active leisure, passive leisure and health. *Economics & Human Biology, 43*, 101053.

Santilli, T. (2025). Inclusion and technological innovation in outdoor learning: Special Pedagogy pathways to co-design augmented reality experiences. *Italian Journal of Health Education, Sports and Inclusive Didactics, 9*(3), 1–18. https://doi.org/10.32043/gsd.v9i3.1604.

Sarmiento-Pelayo M. P. (2015). Co-design: A central approach to the inclusion of people with disabilities. *Revista de la Facultad de Medicina, 63*, 149–154.

Schleien S. J., Germ P. A., McAvoy L. H. (1996). Inclusive community leisure services: Recommended professional practices and barriers encountered. *Therapeutic Recreation Journal, 30*, 260–273.

Schultz, C. S., & McKeown, J. K. (2018). Introduction to the special issue: Toward "digital leisure studies." *Leisure Sciences, 40*(4), 223–238.

Shields, N., & Synnot, A. J. (2016). Perceived barriers and facilitators to participation in physical activity for children with disability: A qualitative study. *BMC Pediatrics, 16*(9), 1–10.

Shogren K. A., Caldarelli A., Del Bianco N., D'Angelo I., Giaconi C. (2022). Co designing inclusive museum itineraries with people with disabilities: A case study from self-determination. *Education Sciences & Society, 2*, 214–226.

Silk, M., Millington, B., Rich, E., & Bush, A. (2019). (Re-) thinking digital leisure. In M. Silk, B. Millington, E. Rich, & A. Bush (Eds.), *Re-thinking Leisure in a Digital Age* (pp. 4–15). Routledge.

Sintas, J. L., De Francisco, L. R., & Álvarez, E. G. (2015). The nature of leisure revisited: An interpretation of digital leisure. *Journal of Leisure Research, 47*(1), 79–101.

Steen, M. (2013). Co-design as a process of joint inquiry and imagination. *Design Issues, 29*(2), 16–28.

Steinhardt, F., Ullenhag, A., Jahnsen, R., & Dolva, A. S. (2021). Perceived facilitators and barriers for participation in leisure activities in children with disabilities: Perspectives of children, parents and professionals. *Scandinavian Journal of Occupational Therapy, 28*(2), 121–135.

Titchkosky, T. (2011). *The question of access.* Space, Meaning, Toronto, University of Toronto Press.

Tokarski, W., & Zarotis, G. F. (2020). Definition, concepts and research about leisure time. *International Journal of Innovative Research and Knowledge, 5*(2), 139–149.

Tribe, J. (2020). *The economics of recreation, leisure and tourism* (6th ed.). Routledge.

United Nations. (2006). Convention on the rights of persons with disabilities. *Treaty Series, 2515*(3), 2006.

Westin, T., Bierre, K., Gramenos, D., & Hinn, M. (2011). Advances in Game Accessibility from 2005 to 2010. In International conference on universal access in human-computer interaction (pp. 400–409). Berlin, Heidelberg: Springer Berlin Heidelberg.

World Health Organization. (2001). *International classification of functioning, disability and health : ICF*. World Health Organization.

World Leisure Organisation, Charter for Leisure (2020) https://www.worldleisure.org/wlo2019/wp-content/uploads/2021/07/Charter-for-Leisure_en.pdf, (2/25).

Yalon-Chamovitz, S., & Weiss, P. L. T. (2008). Virtual reality as a leisure activity for young adults with physical and intellectual disabilities. *Research in Developmental Disabilities, 29*(3), 273–287.

Yuan, B., Folmer, E., & Harris, F. C., Jr. (2011). Game accessibility: A survey. *Universal Access in the Information Society, 10*(1), 81–100.

Chapter 7
A Comprehensive Reading of Theoretical Frameworks

Abstract This final chapter offers an integrative synthesis of the conceptual frameworks developed throughout the book. Drawing on the Grounded Theory approach introduced in Chap. 2, it reconnects the empirical insights emerging from Chaps. 3 to 6 into a comprehensive interpretative framework. The chapter foregrounds the dynamic interplay between fixed and changing design approaches as a defining condition of contemporary game design practice. By revisiting the analyses of process (Chap. 3), artistic expression (Chap. 4), ethics (Chap. 5), and accessibility and inclusion (Chap. 6), it identifies three transversal and intersecting axes (aesthetics, ethics, and inclusion) conceptualised as permeable and mutually influencing dimensions within the design process. The chapter demonstrates how designers continuously negotiate stability and experimentation, convergence and divergence, predictability and innovation. As fixed approaches tend to ensure reliability and control, while changing approaches enable artistic exploration and inclusive potential, albeit with greater uncertainty and ethical complexity. Ultimately, the synthesis argues that effective game design does not reside in privileging one approach over the other, but in responsibly managing their tension in relation to context, objectives, and users.

7.1 Models and Intersections: A Conceptual Snapshot

This final chapter brings together the conceptual frameworks developed throughout the volume in order to offer an integrative synthesis of the perspectives that have emerged from the analysis of game designers' practices. Rather than introducing a new model or advancing a prescriptive stance, the chapter reflects on the relationships, intersections, and tensions that have consistently surfaced across the book, with particular attention to the dynamic interplay between fixed and changing approaches to design. The final framework is shown in Fig. 7.1, and is described in the following paragraphs.

As outlined in Chap. 2, the methodological choice to adopt a Grounded Theory approach has allowed conceptual categories to emerge directly from designers' narrations. This bottom-up perspective revealed that game design practice cannot be

M. Mengoni et al., *Digital Game Design*, https://doi.org/10.1007/978-3-032-23320-2_7

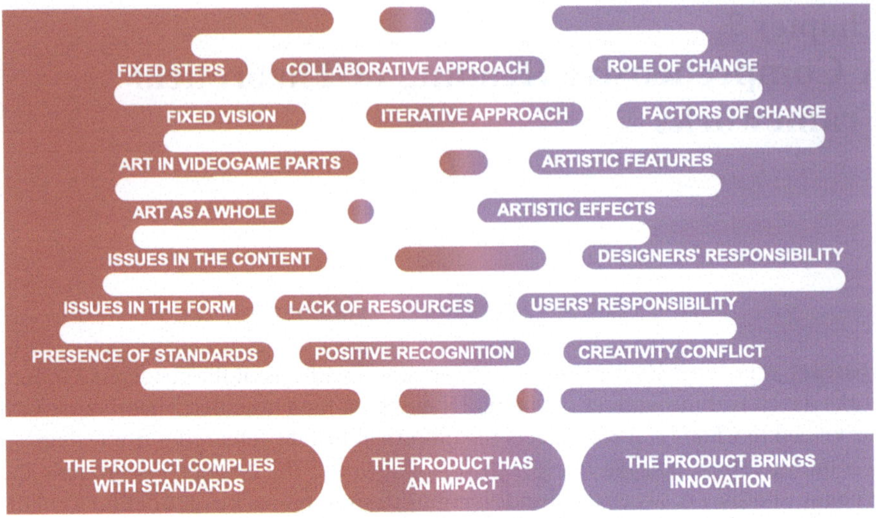

Fig. 7.1 Comprehensive conceptual framework representing a synthesis of game designers' perspectives on all topics examined throughout the book (i.e., design process, art, ethics, and inclusion)

adequately described through linear or static models. Instead, the analyses presented in Chaps. 3–6 consistently point towards a design landscape characterised by movement, negotiation, and balance between opposing tendencies. This concluding chapter aims to make that landscape explicit by reconnecting the various conceptual frameworks into a unified interpretative structure.

A first level of synthesis can be described as a "conceptual snapshot" of the models developed across the volume. Chapters 3–6 each focus on a specific dimension of game design, process, artistic expression, ethics, and accessibility, yet these dimensions repeatedly intersect in designers' accounts. When considered together, they delineate three overarching and transversal axes: aesthetics, ethics, and inclusion. As discussed in Chap. 4, aesthetics emerges not merely as a stylistic concern, but as a dimension closely tied to designers' creative intentions and visions of games as expressive artefacts. Chapter 5 shows how ethical considerations permeate design decisions at multiple levels, from content and representation to economic models and player responsibility. Chapter 6 further extends this reflection by framing accessibility and inclusion as integral aspects of game design, deeply connected to values, professional agency, and social participation. In this synthesis, these three dimensions can be envisioned as spheres embedded within a permeable membrane representing the design process itself. The permeability of this membrane reflects the continuous flow between fixed and changing approaches identified in Chap. 3. Aesthetics, ethics, and inclusion do not occupy fixed positions; rather, they shift and reconfigure depending on context, constraints, and design intentions. Their intersection forms a shared conceptual space in which designers negotiate priorities and responsibilities throughout the development process.

7.1.1 Processes and Approaches: From Fixed to Changing

The tension between fixed and changing approaches, introduced and theorised in Chap. 3, constitutes a central thread running through the entire volume. Chapter 3 conceptualises game design as a balance between permanence and change, highlighting how designers rely on stable structures and shared conventions while remaining open to iteration, transformation, and uncertainty. When design practice moves from a fixed towards a changing approach, the process becomes increasingly exploratory and adaptive. Fixed approaches are associated with established pipelines, standardised mechanics, and predictable outcomes, often aligning with the expectations discussed in Chap. 3 regarding stability and coherence. These approaches tend to ensure functional correctness, usability, and aesthetic consistency, echoing concerns raised in Chap. 5 about responsibility and control. Conversely, changing approaches privilege experimentation and innovation. As reflected in Chap. 4, such approaches often enable stronger forms of artistic expression, allowing designers to push aesthetic boundaries and explore unconventional solutions. Similarly, Chap. 6 shows how changing approaches can open space for rethinking accessibility and inclusion, albeit with increased uncertainty and dependency on designers' awareness, competence, and organisational support. Importantly, designers' narrations rarely align exclusively with one end of the continuum. Instead, as evidenced across all empirical chapters, movement between fixed and changing approaches occurs continuously and bidirectionally, depending on the phase of development, the target audience, and contextual constraints.

7.2 Results and Impacts of Design Approaches

The comparative analysis developed throughout the volume highlights how different approaches lead to distinct types of outcomes. As suggested in Chap. 3, fixed approaches tend to generate predictable and convergent results, particularly suitable for projects prioritising efficiency, scalability, and adherence to recognised standards. This predictability is often perceived by designers as a form of professional safety, reducing risks associated with production constraints or user expectations.

Changing approaches, by contrast, are associated with outcomes that designers describe as more surprising, expressive, and potentially innovative. Chapter 4 illustrates how artistic value often emerges from such approaches, while Chap. 6 indicates that inclusive solutions may arise through non-standard design choices that challenge established practices. However, as discussed in Chap. 5, these outcomes also raise ethical questions, as unpredictability can amplify both positive and negative impacts on players. Across the chapters, most designers describe their practice as a continuous negotiation between these two modes. The resulting tension is not portrayed as a problem to be resolved, but as a defining feature of professional game design.

7.2.1 Balancing Opposites: Fears and Opportunities

Designers' reflections reveal that the fixed–changing tension is experienced not only at a procedural level, but also at an emotional and motivational one. As highlighted in Chap. 3, fixed approaches are often associated with security, control, and confidence in meeting expectations. Changing approaches, on the other hand, are linked to creative ambition, experimentation, and personal challenge. This duality resonates with the broader distinction between convergence and divergence that runs implicitly across the volume. Fixed approaches tend towards convergence, producing expected and recognisable outcomes, while changing approaches embrace divergence, opening up the possibility of the unexpected. As Chap. 5 suggests, this divergence can be ethically productive but also ethically risky, requiring designers to remain reflexive about the consequences of their choices. Managing this balance emerges as a key aspect of designers' professional agency. Rather than choosing between safety and innovation, designers continuously navigate both, adjusting their positioning in response to project goals, team dynamics, and user needs.

7.2.2 Concluding Reflections

The synthesis developed in this chapter reinforces a central insight of the volume: there is no universally optimal approach to digital game design. As consistently demonstrated across Chaps. 3–6, design practices are shaped by a complex interplay of objectives, constraints, values, and contexts. The balance between fixed and changing approaches is therefore not a matter of choice, but an ongoing condition of professional practice. The challenge for designers lies in managing this tension responsibly, integrating aesthetic ambition (Chap. 4), ethical awareness (Chap. 5), and inclusive intent (Chap. 6) within coherent and context-sensitive design processes. By articulating these tensions through empirically grounded conceptual frameworks, the volume invites designers and researchers alike to reflect critically on their own positioning, practices, and assumptions. In doing so, Digital Games Design: Voices, Values and Visions does not seek to close the discussion on game design, but to open a space for continued dialogue between theory and practice—one that acknowledges uncertainty as a productive force and responsibility as a central dimension of creative work.

Appendix A
Interview Questions

(1) Participants' personal data	Place of birth Gender Age Education Years of experience Role Affiliation	
(2) Design thinking	How many design projects have you approached in your professional experience?	Which projects have you developed?
	When considering a design project, are there specific steps that you follow in your design workflow? What comes first?	
	If so, how flexible are these steps in terms of the specificity of the project? Are these steps common to all projects? And what determines the flexibility?	
(3) Idea generation	How do you frame a design case?	When framing a design case, do you adopt a narrow vision (focusing on the individual aspects you want to achieve) or do you adopt a wider vision?
	How do you deal with User Needs in your design process?	The design industry's attention shifted from UI to the wider concept of UX. Did this happen for game design as well? or has UX always been preeminent in game design, under the form of gameplay?

(continued)

M. Mengoni et al., *Digital Game Design*, https://doi.org/10.1007/978-3-032-23320-2

(continued)

		What do you think is the relationship between UX and UI? What comes first?
	What are the primary sources of inspiration and stimuli that provide you with ideas for a project?	Do you think the design solutions adopted by other designers influence your work?
		Do you think the design solutions you previously adopted in your professional experience influence your work?
(4) Idea development and concept	Which software tools do you use in your work?	
	In the process of development of an idea, what influences the aesthetics, the choice of graphic style?	What influences the choice of 2D style or 3D style?
	In your opinion, what makes a game a work of art?	
	How does the working context affect the development of an idea?	
	How do external limits (such as budget, time, etc.) affect the development of an idea?	How did you overcome such limits?
	Do any ethical aspects emerge in your projects? How do you deal with the ethical dimension of video games? Do you wonder how it influences its outcomes?	
(5) User, inclusion & accessibility	Do you consider users' ability when designing a game?	
	How do you conceptualise accessibility, usability and engagement? What do they mean to you and what role do they play in your design process?	
	Do you think the game industry gives enough attention to the theme of inclusion and diversity of its final users?	What do you suggest?

(continued)

(continued)

(6) Conclusion	How do you think the interaction modalities of digital games will be reshaped in the future, considering the new emerging technologies?	
	What did you learn from your professional experience?	Is there a specific story (fun, good, bad) that you would like to share from which you have learned something valuable for your profession?

Appendix B
Designers Profiles

M. Mengoni et al., *Digital Game Design*, https://doi.org/10.1007/978-3-032-23320-2

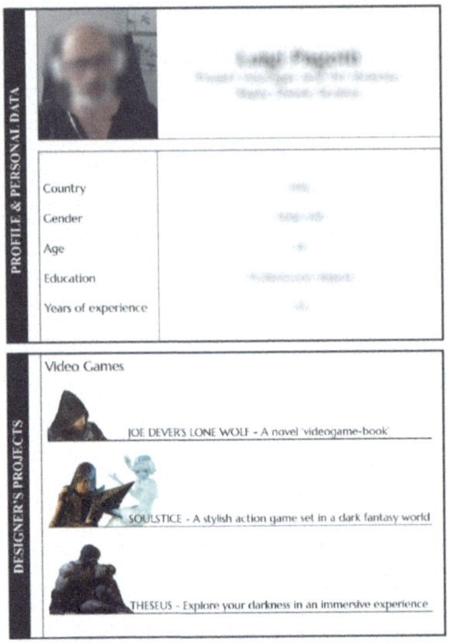
PROFILE & PERSONAL DATA
Country
Gender
Age
Education
Years of experience
DESIGNER'S PROJECTS
Video Games
JOE DEVER'S LONE WOLF - A novel 'videogame-book'
SOULSTICE - A stylish action game set in a dark fantasy world
THESEUS - Explore your darkness in an immersive experience

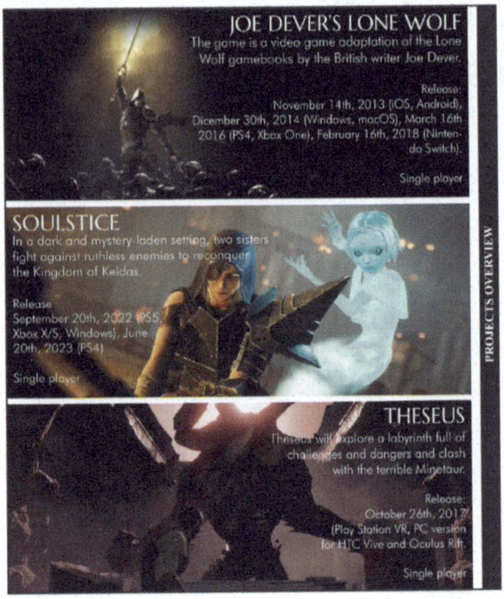
JOE DEVER'S LONE WOLF
The game is a video game adaptation of the Lone Wolf gamebooks by the British writer Joe Dever.
Release:
November 14th, 2013 (iOS, Android), Dicember 30th, 2014 (Windows, macOS), March 16th 2016 (PS4, Xbox One), February 16th, 2018 (Nintendo Switch).
Single player
SOULSTICE
In a dark and mystery-laden setting, two sisters fight against ruthless enemies to reconquer the Kingdom of Keidas.
Release
September 20th, 2022 (PS5, Xbox X/S, Windows), June 20th, 2023 (PS4)
Single player
THESEUS
Theseus will explore a labyrinth full of challenges and dangers and clash with the terrible Minotaur.
Release:
October 26th, 2017 (Play Station VR, PC version for HTC Vive and Oculus Rift.
Single player
PROJECTS OVERVIEW

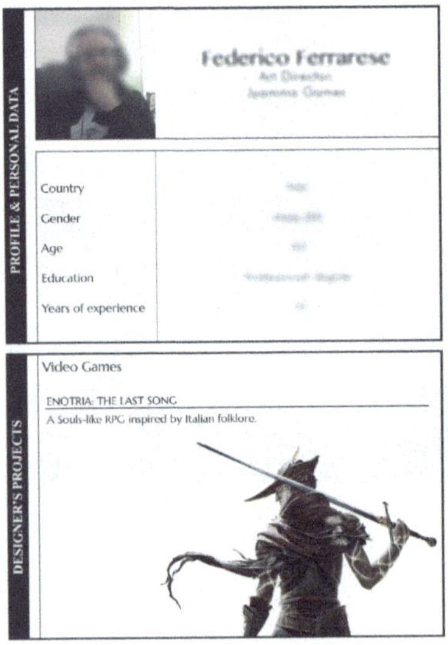
PROFILE & PERSONAL DATA
Federico Ferrarese
Country
Gender
Age
Education
Years of experience
DESIGNER'S PROJECTS
Video Games
ENOTRIA: THE LAST SONG
A Souls-like RPG inspired by Italian folklore.

ENOTRIA: THE LAST GAME
It is a Souls-like action RPG set in a fantasy world based on Italian folklore and culture. The game aims to take the genre in a new direction, where gameplay allows you to alter the world and enemies in a systemic way.
Release:
September 30th, 2024 (Windows, PS5,), Dicember 12th 2024 (Xbox X/S), Single player
PROJECTS OVERVIEW

PROFILE & PERSONAL DATA
Country
Gender
Age
Education
Years of experience
DESIGNER'S PROJECTS
Video Games
JOE DEVER'S LONE WOLF - A novel 'videogame-book'
SOULSTICE - A stylish action game set in a dark fantasy world
THESEUS - Explore your darkness in an immersive experience
PROJECTS OVERVIEW
JOE DEVER'S LONE WOLF
The game is a video game adaptation of the Lone Wolf gamebooks by the British writer Joe Dever.
Release:
November 14th, 2013 (iOS, Android), Dicember 30th, 2014 (Windows, macOS), March 16th 2016 (PS4, Xbox One), February 16th, 2018 (Nintendo Switch)
Single player
SOULSTICE
In a dark and mystery-laden setting, two sisters fight against ruthless enemies to reconquer the Kingdom of Keidas.
Release
September 20th, 2022 (PS5, Xbox X/S, Windows), June 20th, 2023 (PS4)
Single player
THESEUS
Theseus will explore a labyrinth full of challenges and dangers and clash with the terrible Minotaur.
Release:
October 26th, 2017
(Play Station VR, PC version for HTC Vive and Oculus Rift
Single player
PROFILE & PERSONAL DATA
Country
Gender
Age
Education
Years of experience
DESIGNER'S PROJECTS
Video Games
FREUD'S BONES - A journey into Freud's brain
EMPTY - Dealing with mindfulness eating
BLUETHROOT - The brutal age
WORKDOWN - Is there a place for mental health at work?
PROJECTS OVERVIEW
FREUD'S BONES
Freud's Bones is the first video game concerning Freudian psychoanalysis and existential crisis.
Release:
May 25th, 2022 on Windows,
November 24th, 2022 on Nintendo Switch.
Single player
EMPTY
Empty is a 3D narrative adventure dealing with the theme of mindfulness eating.
Demo available on itch.io
Single player
BLUETHROOT
Bluethroot is an unprecedented video game about adolescence and its demons.
Release:
January 24th, 2024 on Windows.
Single player
WORKDOWN
The first video game about mental health in business. The main character will embark on an inner journey to discover himself and his mental well-being.
Demo available on Game2Value
Single player

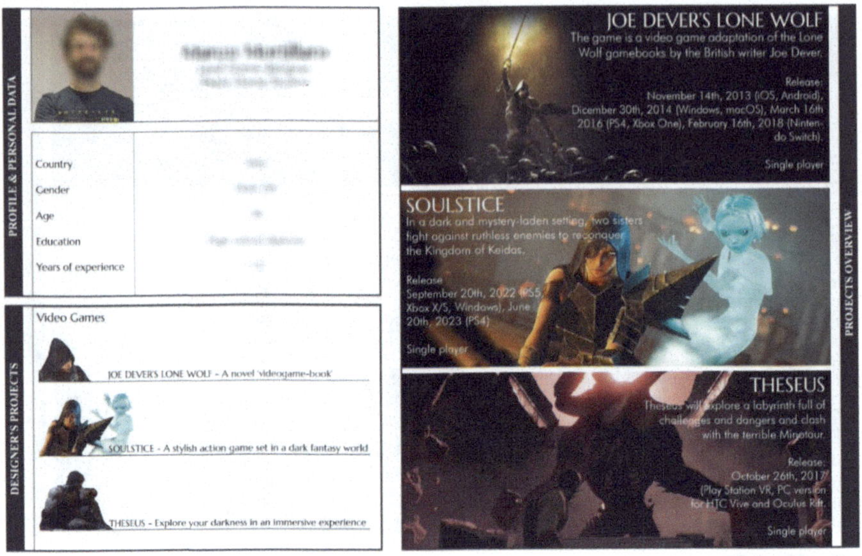
PROFILE & PERSONAL DATA
Country
Gender
Age
Education
Years of experience
DESIGNER'S PROJECTS
Video Games
JOE DEVER'S LONE WOLF - A novel 'videogame-book'
SOULSTICE - A stylish action game set in a dark fantasy world
THESEUS - Explore your darkness in an immersive experience
PROJECTS OVERVIEW
JOE DEVER'S LONE WOLF
The game is a video game adaptation of the Lone Wolf gamebooks by the British writer Joe Dever.
Release:
November 14th, 2013 (iOS, Android), Dicember 30th, 2014 (Windows, macOS), March 16th 2016 (PS4, Xbox One), February 16th, 2018 (Nintendo Switch).
Single player
SOULSTICE
In a dark and mystery-laden setting, two sisters fight against ruthless enemies to reconquer the Kingdom of Keidas.
Release
September 20th, 2022 (PS5, Xbox X/S, Windows), June 20th, 2023 (PS4)
Single player
THESEUS
Theseus will explore a labyrinth full of challenges and dangers and clash with the terrible Minotaur.
Release:
October 26th, 2017
(Play Station VR, PC version for HTC Vive and Oculus Rift.
Single player

Appendix C
Complete List of Codes

- Pre-design
  - Conceiving and defining a concept
  - Analysing feasibility of the project
- Planning the game development
- Designing and prototyping
- Testing
- Starting from an overall view to progressively define smaller parts of the game
- Focusing of details first is counterproductive
- Considering that game design practices vary through time, among teams and among different approaches
- Highlighting the importance of flexibility of the game design process
- Seeing challenges of game design as opportunities
- Starting from an overall view to progressively define smaller parts of the game
- Focusing of details first is counterproductive
- Considering that game design practices vary through time, among teams and among different approaches
- Highlighting the importance of flexibility of the game design process
- Seeing challenges of game design as opportunities
- Market
- Budget
- Time
- Stakeholders' requests
- Team composition
- Importance of team communication
- Importance of combining individual talents
- Sharing and preserving an overall view of the game
- Assessing design ideas
- Avoiding tunnel vision effects
- Video games are a product of creativity
- Video games can narrate a story

M. Mengoni et al., *Digital Game Design*, https://doi.org/10.1007/978-3-032-23320-2

- Video games combine technology and artistic language
- Video games give users freedom of expression
- Video games can generate escapism
- Video games can stimulate reflection
- Video games can evoke emotions
- Video games can trigger learning
- Graphic style
- Soundtrack
- Game mechanics
- User Interface
- Video game as collective art
- Video game as interactive art
- Inputs for reflection and awareness-raising
- Not all games contain ethical issues
- Choices and fruition modalities
- Designers' responsibility should be acknowledged
- Designers' responsibility should not be overarching
- Users have responsibility
- Perceiving accessibility as a responsibility and means for social inclusion
- Considering accessibility as a dimension that concerns all
- Recognising the relevance of existing standards
- Complying to standards as minimum baseline
- Perceiving accessibility as a limit to creativity
- Not considering accessibility as a priority
- Recognising constraints related to accessibility implementation

The manufacturer's authorised representative in the EU is Springer Nature Customer Service Centre GmbH, Europaplatz 3, 69115 Heidelberg, Germany. If you have any concerns regarding our products, please contact ProductSafety@springernature.com

Printed and bound by CPI Group (UK) Ltd, Croydon, CR0 4YY
05/10/2026
02228059-0002